English ⌗ Heritage
Book of
Roman York

English ⌗ Heritage
Book of
Roman York

Patrick Ottaway

B. T. Batsford Ltd/English Heritage
London

This book is dedicated to the city and people of York

First published 1993

Typeset by Lasertext Ltd, Stretford,
Manchester M32 0JT
and printed in Great Britain by
The Bath Press, Bath

Published by B T Batsford Ltd
4 Fitzhardinge Street, London W1H 0AH

A CIP catalogue record for this book is
available from the British Library

ISBN 0 7134 7082 8 (cased)
0 7134 7083 6 (limp)

Contents

Illustrations

Colour plates

Acknowledgements

In preparing this book I have been given the most generous support and encouragement by my colleagues at York Archaeological Trust. I am particularly grateful to Peter Addyman and Richard Hall, and I also wish to express thanks to Glenys Boyles, Martin Brann, Amanda Clarke, Hilary Cool, Rhona Finlayson, Jason Monaghan, Niall Oakey and Nick Pearson. In addition, I owe a special debt of gratitude to Terry Finnemore who drew illustrations 8, 9, 22, 27, and checked every detail on the fortress plan.

Beyond the confines of the Archaeological Trust I am most grateful to Martin Millett of Durham University who read through the draft text and made many useful comments and suggestions.

My thanks are also due to Elizabeth Hartley, Keeper of Archaeology at the Yorkshire Museum for making illustrations of items in the collections available. Allan Hall, Andrew Jones, Harry Kenward, Terry O'Connor, past and present fellows of the University of York Environmental Archaeology Unit have kindly provided information on matters concerning their specialist interests. In developing ideas on the planning of the legionary fortress I have been greatly assisted by the advice of Philip Crummy, Director of Colchester Archaeological Trust.

The recent excavations on which much of this account of Roman York is based have been generously funded over many years by the Department of the Environment, English Heritage and York City Council. Substantial and much appreciated contributions have also been made for specific projects by General Accident Assurance, Stakis Hotels and Vignor Ltd.

Simon Hill of York Archaeological Trust was responsible for new photographs for the book (back cover and 49, 67, 71, and **colour plates 9** and **12**). **Colour plates 1, 4, 7, 11** and **13** were taken by Jim Kershaw. Other photographs were taken by Keith Buck, Mike Duffy and members of the Archaeological Trust photography department. Colour illustrations **2** and **10** were prepared by Tracey Croft of English Heritage. Line illustrations **4, 7, 16, 26**b, **34, 37, 39, 60** and **72** were drawn by David Williams. The remaining line illustrations were drawn as follows: **12** by Sheena Howarth, **40** by Peter Marshall, **26**a, **54** and **59** by Dick Raines, **33** by Glenys Boyles, **42** by Helen Humphreys, **43** by Anne Thomas and **62** by Trevor Pearson.

I am grateful to the following for permission to use copyright illustrations:
Dr A. Crawshaw (**colour plate 3**)
The Dean and Chapter of York (**colour plate 7**)
Dr R.F.J. Jones (**5–6**)
The Royal Commission on Historical Monuments (England) (**20, 31, 47, 52, 53, 55** and **56**)
The Yorkshire Museum (back cover, **3, 49, colour plates 1, 4, 11, 12** and **13**)

Dates
The periods of York's history referred to in this book are dated as follows:
Roman: 71–c.410
Anglian: c.410–850
Anglo-Scandinavian: c.850–1066
Medieval: c.1066–1485

Measurements
Measurements are given in metric followed by imperial equivalents in brackets. Discussions

ACKNOWLEDGEMENTS

of the metrology of the Roman fortress are usually conducted in terms of the standard Roman foot (*pes Monetalis*) with imperial and metre equivalents. 1pM = 0.296 m or 0.97 of an imperial foot.

Heights above sea level are indicated as OD, Ordnance Datum.

Spelling of the Roman name for York

The Roman name for York is spelt *Eboracum* by the geographer Ptolemy and in several inscriptions from the city, whereas the spelling *Eburacum* is to be found in the Antonine Itinerary and Ravenna Cosmography, and on one inscription. The former spelling has been used in this book. The name may derive from a British word meaning 'place of yews'.

1

The search for Roman York – 'a place of great importance'

For an overall plan of Roman York and location of extramural sites see **1**; for a plan showing sites in the fortress see **8**; in the civilian settlement north-east of the Ouse see **32**; and in the civilian settlement south-west of the Ouse see **33**.

The City of York, known to the Romans as *Eboracum* (or *Eburacum*), owes its origins to the ninth legion who arrived there in AD 71 and built a great fortress on the north-east bank of the river Ouse. In about 120 the ninth was replaced by the sixth who remained as the garrisoning force until the end of the Roman period in the early fifth century. During the second century York also became the site of a major urban settlement. One part lay on the north-east bank of the Ouse, and the other on the south-west bank. By the early third century this had acquired the status of a *colonia* indicating that its inhabitants were considered worthy of carrying the sacred flame of Roman civilization to the barbarous north. This dual character, with military and civilian sites of the highest rank side by side, makes *Eboracum* unique in Britain and crucial for the understanding of the Roman imperial achievement in this country.

The two best-known episodes in the history of Roman York are the visit in 209–11 of the Emperor Septimius Severus, which culminated in his death, and the acclamation of Constantine I ('the Great') as emperor in 306, following the death of his father Constantius I, the city's second imperial casualty. These great events which thrust York on to the world's stage have given an added edge to local pride, leading William Hargrove, for example, to open his *History of York* published in 1818 as follows:

In the earliest records of English History, Ebor, Eboracum, or York, is represented as a place of great importance; and, in the zenith of meridian splendour, it was the residence of Imperial Power, and the legislative seat of the Roman Empire. Hence we may readily suppose, especially when the ancient historic accounts of this city are contrasted with those of London, that York far exceeded in dignity and consequence, if not in population and extent, the present capital of the British Empire, at that period.

While such hyperbole is out of fashion today, the Roman period still captures the imagination at least as powerfully as any other period of York's history; indeed, the status it acquired in the late first century has coloured almost every aspect of the City's subsequent development. After Britain had ceased to be part of the Roman Empire York was to retain a pre-eminent role in the economic, military, political and religious affairs of the north of England in the succeeding Anglian, Anglo-Scandinavian and medieval periods. Although it has to be admitted that York's economic and political dominance had begun to decline by the end of Elizabeth I's reign, the church and the army have retained York as their northern headquarters to the present day. In the mid-nineteenth century York returned to a position of regional economic importance as a railway centre and during the reign of Elizabeth II it has become a thriving city of some 100,000 inhabitants with a diverse economy based not only on engineering and the manufacture of confectionery, but also on tourism, the basis of which is the history briefly outlined above.

It is, of course, in the nature of things that

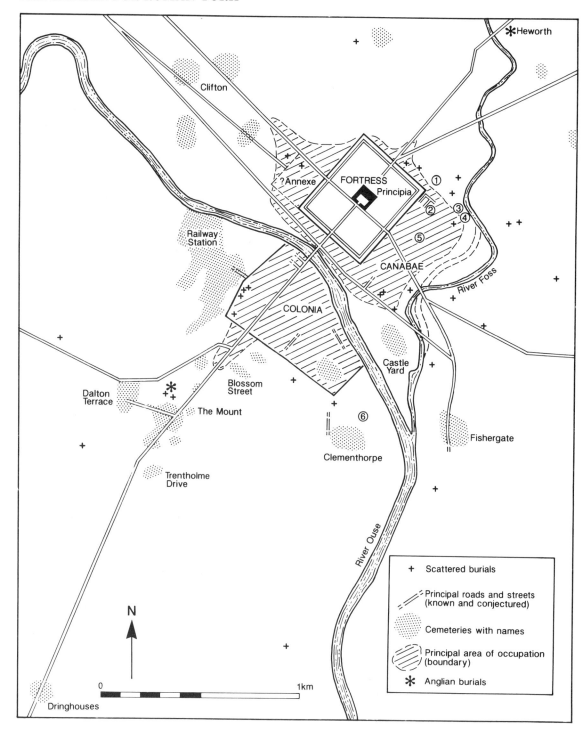

1 *Roman York and its environs showing the principal areas of settlement, cemeteries (known) and roads and streets (known and conjectured).*

Key to extramural sites: 1 County Hospital; 2 21–33 Aldwark (Ebor Brewery); 3 Borthwick Institute; 4 Peaseholme Green (Adams Hydraulics); 5 Conjectured site of amphitheatre; 6 Clementhorpe.

a place which has been occupied for such a long period should see the buildings, streets and monuments of one generation demolished and built over by the next. As a result, there is little of Roman York to be seen above ground today, but a flavour of former glories can still be enjoyed at three locations in the former fortress. At its very heart, displayed where they were unearthed during restoration of the Minster tower, can be seen the remains of the *principia* or headquarters building. At the east corner of the fortress stands the fine walling of the defences which may date to the reign of Septimius Severus (see **23**) and, finally, in the Museum Gardens is the Multangular Tower (**colour plate 9**), marking the west corner of the fortress, which together with the adjacent stretches of the curtain wall, forms one of the most impressive witnesses to the military power of the Roman empire to be found anywhere in western Europe. In addition, the nearby Yorkshire Museum boasts a remarkable collection of Roman antiquities ranging from fine stone sculpture to grave finds such as pottery vessels and jewellery made of bone, jet and precious metals.

There are no other upstanding Roman remains in York, but the medieval city walls to the north-east and north-west of the Minster overlie the defences of the fortress, while two of York's principal thoroughfares, Stonegate and Petergate, are on the line of important fortress streets. South-west of the Ouse the medieval walls are also likely to overlie Roman defences.

In the virtual absence of contemporary written references, archaeological discoveries form the archive on which any account of Roman York must depend. Since much of this archive is buried and unseen, however, it is worth outlining some of its characteristics by way of an introduction to the discoveries themselves. The archaeology of York is made up, firstly, of abandoned structures in varying states of incompleteness and, secondly, of a vast number of superimposed layers of building debris, domestic and industrial refuse, ancient garden soil and the like which are testimony to the intensity of human activity in the city over the centuries. These layers typically survive to a depth of 2–3 m (6½–10 ft), but in places the ground surface as it was before the arrival of man may be as much as 10 m (33 ft) below the modern level. The depth of buried structures

and deposits poses serious technical problems for archaeologists, requiring, for example, the use of expensive shoring to keep trench sides safe. The remains of the Roman period, usually buried more deeply than those of later times, are, however, relatively well preserved from damage by modern intrusions such as cellars and service trenches. Another factor favouring preservation arises from York's low-lying situation which means that it has been greatly affected by the gradual rise of the water-table since Roman times. In many areas of the city archaeological layers have become waterlogged and this has ensured the remarkable and unusual survival of organic materials, from timber buildings to ancient meals.

Although the archaeology of York can be seen as an archive, it is, of course, unlike the papers in a library which can be consulted time and time again. Every time we read a page of the buried past in the course of excavation we are essentially destroying it and thorough recording of discoveries is therefore vital. The history of archaeology in York can be considered representative of the subject's history in Britain as a whole. A continuous thread of development links the work of the early antiquaries, who concentrated on the piecemeal recovery of individual objects of intrinsic artistic or historical interest, with the field projects of today which are part of a rigorous academic discipline demanding the highest standards in records and publications.

Roman York – a history of research

As far as the investigation of the Roman period in York is concerned, local interest is recorded as early as 1638 when an altar dedicated to Jupiter was found in Bishophill Senior on the south-west bank of the Ouse. The first scholar of national reputation to draw general attention to the subject, however, was the Tudor geographer and historian William Camden. In his *Britannia*, a unique survey of historical sites and monuments throughout the country, Camden noted such finds as the splendid tombstone of the standard bearer Lucius Duccius Rufinus (**colour plate 1**), found in 1688 at Holy Trinity church, and the stone coffin of Verecundius Diogenes, a *sevir augustalis* (priest of the cult of the deified emperor), apparently found in 1579.

In the eighteenth and nineteenth centuries many distinguished York residents of local and national reputation interested themselves in York's Roman remains. They included Martin Lister (1638?–1712), the eminent zoologist who was a polymath true to the spirit of his times. He contributed papers on such discoveries as the Bishophill altar to the Philosophical Transactions of the Royal Society. Lister was also the first person to recognize the Multangular Tower as a Roman structure and his work formed one of the sources for a great landmark in the study of York's history. Entitled *Eboracum*, but covering all periods, this work was published in 1736 by Francis Drake (1696–1771), a local surgeon. As a correspondent of the great antiquary William Stukeley, creator of much of the mythology of the Druids, Drake, like many other amateur scholars of his time, combined a curiosity about the past and a desire to record its remains, with fanciful speculation and misplaced civic pride. This led him, for example, erroneously to assert that the Emperor Constantine the Great had been born in York.

In 1818, William Hargrove the York newspaper proprietor and journalist, published the history of York quoted earlier which reviewed previous discoveries and added such new material as the Mithraic relief, found in 1747 near St Martin-cum-Gregory church and the temple of Serapis found on Toft Green in 1770 (**2**). The search for *Eboracum* was continued by the Reverend Charles Wellbeloved (1769–1858).

Wellbeloved was also one of the founders of the Yorkshire Philosophical Society and the first honorary curator of antiquities in the Society's museum, known today as the Yorkshire Museum. In 1842 Wellbeloved published his *Eburacum*; based both on previous discoveries and first-hand observation it included the discovery of the fortress defences destroyed during the creation of St Leonard's Place and Exhibition Square in 1835. Wellbeloved also correctly surmised the limits of the legionary fortress – or 'city' as he called it – although they were not finally demonstrated by excavation until the 1950s. In addition, *Eburacum* contains extensive descriptions of discoveries in the 'suburbs' on the south-west bank of the Ouse, notably part of a great baths complex in the north-western part of the *colonia*, the remains of which were revealed during the building of the Old Railway Station in 1839–40. This involved making a breach in the medieval and Roman defences and was probably

2 *Illustration from Wellbeloved's* Eburacum *published 1842. The Mithraic relief (*top) *found in Micklegate in 1747 and the dedication tablet from the temple of Serapis found in Toft Green in 1770. The latter reads: To the holy god Serapis –* DEO SANCTO SERAPI *– Claudius Hieronymianus, legate of the sixth legion victorious, built this temple from the ground –* A SOLO FECIT.

the most devastating single episode of destruction ever suffered by York's archaeology.

A great deal was also destroyed during the latter half of the nineteenth and early twentieth centuries when York grew rapidly as a result of its new-found role as a railway centre. One of the more important discoveries which was recorded, however, was a great commemorative inscription of the reign of Trajan found in King's Square in 1854 during work on York's first main sewers (3). In the 1870s another redoubtable clergyman-antiquary, the Reverend James Raine, curator of antiquities at the Yorkshire Museum between 1873 and 1896, observed the massive earthmoving operations undertaken for the present railway station which disturbed one of the principal cemeteries of the Roman *colonia*. At much the same time, the creation of a fashionable suburb on the Mount outside Micklegate Bar led to the discovery of many more fine funerary monuments which had originally lined the main Roman road to York from the south-west.

The first systematic archaeological excavations in Roman York were conducted in the 1920s under the direction of Stuart Miller, a lecturer at Glasgow University, on behalf of the York Excavation Committee, a body newly formed along the lines of a number of others which emerged in historic towns around Britain at this time. Between 1925 and 1928 Miller addressed himself primarily to the fortress defences and it was while digging at the east corner that he revealed, preserved beneath the medieval rampart, the stretch of fortress wall standing some 5 m (16 ft) high which can still be seen today.

During the 1950s and 1960s, a time of increasing redevelopment in the city, much of the burden of investigating York's archaeology was borne by volunteers with restricted resources. One of the most active excavators of the period was Peter Wenham, head of history at St John's College. His work included investigation of the site of the Davygate shopping arcade from 1955 to 1958 where he recorded the fortress defences and four legionary barrack blocks (which he designated, appropriately, S, P, Q and R!). Wenham's most extensive excavation, however, took place at Trentholme Drive, about half a mile south-west of Micklegate Bar, where he found a substantial Roman cemetery, the first in York to be scientifically examined rather than unearthed in building work.

Archaeological work in York in the 1950s was also undertaken by the staff of the Royal Commission on Historical Monuments as part of their great inventory of the city. The first volume, *Eburacum*, which appeared in 1962, is a thorough catalogue and evaluation of all discoveries of the Roman period made up to that date. It remains a vital source for research on Roman York, although its conclusions now require modification in many respects. The Royal Commission was also involved in excavations at the Minster in the heart of the fortress, where the danger of collapse of the central tower rendered major ground works necessary. Archaeological work began in 1967 and was completed in 1972 by Derek Phillips who became the York Minster archaeologist. Initially the aim of the Minster excavations was to locate the Anglo-Saxon minster referred to by Bede as the site of King Edwin of Northumbria's baptism in 627. As time went on, however, and Edwin's church did not appear, other research interests, including the Roman *principia*, were given attention, especially when it was decided that the Roman walls should be put on public display. Although work could only proceed in small areas during restoration and conditions were difficult, if not dangerous, the complete sequence of development of the headquarters basilica and the adjacent barracks was discovered.

While work was beginning at the Minster, the Commission had moved on to the next volume of its York inventory which was concerned with the city's defences. In connection with this work Jeffrey Radley set about re-excavating a stone tower (see **67**) built up against the Roman fortress wall near the Multangular Tower. This was first discovered in 1842, when the Recorder of York had driven a tunnel through it to get access to his stables in King's Manor. Radley suggested that the tower was post-Roman and it is now officially known as the 'Anglian Tower', although for reasons which will be discussed below (pp.109–11, the tower is more likely to be late Roman. Subsequent to the excavation York City Council decided to put the tower on permanent display and, in addition, as part of the celebrations which took place in 1971 to commemorate 1900 years of York since its foundation by the Romans, exposed an adjacent stretch of the fortress wall by removing the overlying medieval rampart.

In spite of the discoveries outlined above, the overall picture of archaeological work in York in the late 1960s and early 1970s was one of an inadequate response to the threat posed by modern development. Projects were dealt with on an individual basis and there was no body with overall strategic or academic responsibility. The 'rescue' crisis in York acquired a

3 *The commemorative inscription found in King's Square. It is the last dated reference to the ninth legion and can be ascribed to the year December 107 to December 108. The dedication to Trajan gives his titles as Emperor Caesar, son of the divine Nerva, Nerva Traianus Augustus, Germanicus, Dacicus,* pontifex maximus *— IM]P(ERATOR) CAESAR DIVI [N]ERVAE FIL (IVS) N[ERVA TRAI]ANVS AVG(VSTVS) GER[M(ANICVS) DACICVS [PO]NTIFEX MAXIMV[S.*

Dating is derived from reference to the fact that Trajan was in his twelfth year of tribunician power, fifth year as imperator and fifth year as consul — TRIBVNICIAE [PO]TESTATIS XII IMP(ERATOR) V [CO(N)S(VL) V. Reference to the legion is in the last line where the work commemorated is described as — PER LEG(IONEM) VIIII HI[SP(ANAM) FECIT.

16

new urgency in 1968 with the publication of Lord Esher's report entitled *York: A Study in Conservation* which led to plans for an inner ring-road. While it was the intention to avoid above-ground historic buildings, the road threatened large areas of rich below-ground archaeology immediately outside the city walls, including Roman cemeteries and suburbs. At this point the Council for British Archaeology and the Yorkshire Philosophical Society, the latter imbued no doubt with the spirit of its founder member the Reverend Charles Well-beloved, sponsored the formation of the York Archaeological Trust (YAT). This was set up in April 1972 with funds from the Department of the Environment and assistance and premises from York University.

The Trust is an organization comparable to a number of others set up at about the same time to tackle archaeology in major historic towns. Their work involves, in the first instance, excavation in advance of new building and other construction work, and the monitoring of all other disturbances of the ground caused by service trenches and the like. Fieldwork in York has, however, been further guided by specific research objectives within what Trust Director, Peter Addyman, has described as a 'broadly based examination of the whole process of urbanisation over the past two millennia'. The study of Roman York has, of course, had a major part to play in this and since 1972 a wide range of projects has added enormously to our understanding of the subject. A brief summary may serve to prepare the reader for more detailed discussion in the following chapters.

Recent excavations
As far as the Roman fortress is concerned, work has, as before, been mostly small scale, but has included further examination of the defences and adjacent areas near the east corner in the Aldwark/Bedern area in advance of the urban renewal proposed by Esher. In the central part of the fortress rescue work in Church Street in 1972 revealed the great sewer which served the bath house, and an excavation at 9 Blake Street (the former City Garage, now Stonegate Walk) in 1975 produced a sequence of buildings and an internal street. Although large areas of the fortress will remain inaccessible for archaeological examination below the historic buildings of the city centre, the small sites and

watching briefs of the last 20 years have allowed much of the basic plan of the late first-century fortress to be determined along with aspects of the changes in layout which took place in the second century.

Study of the Roman civilian settlements has been concentrated on the opposite bank of the Ouse to the fortress, and has formed one of the Trust's most coherent research projects within the rescue framework. This began in 1973 with the examination of the remains of a large town house sited on an artificial terrace in the south-eastern part of the *colonia* at 37 Bishophill Senior. On the adjacent 58–9 Skeldergate site a remarkably well-preserved timber-lined well was discovered (see **54**). Its conservation had an important part to play in the development of techniques for the treatment of waterlogged wood from archaeological sites, in which the YAT conservation laboratory has become an internationally recognized authority. In addition, the contents of the well were highly organic and included abundant plant remains, animal bones and even micro-organisms from the human gut. This material provided one of the first indications of the potential in York for understanding the ecology of Roman urbanism and the subject has been one of the principal research themes of the Environmental Archaeology Unit established by YAT and the Inspectorate of Ancient Monuments at York University.

My own involvement with the archaeology of Roman York began in 1981 with a small trench in the *colonia* at 5 Rougier Street, close to the main Roman road from the south-west. The site produced some 3 m (10 ft) of Roman deposits and demonstrated the existence of a well-preserved buried Roman townscape in this hitherto unexplored part of the city. In 1983–4 more extensive trenches were dug in the same area, under the direction of Nick Pearson, in advance of an extension to the offices of General Accident Assurance on the corner of Rougier Street and Tanner Row. This was one of the first excavations in York to receive substantial funding from the site developers themselves. Previously, funding for the Trust's work had been largely provided by central government, but in recent years it has become the norm at York, in line with practice elsewhere in the country, for developers to bear the principal cost burden of rescue archaeology.

The Tanner Row site produced remarkable remains of late second-century timber buildings with their associated artefact-rich refuse heaps. The trenches here were narrow, however, and complete building plans could not be determined. Fortunately, a much larger area became available in May 1988 at the nearby Wellington Row site where I directed excavations for much of the next $2\frac{1}{2}$ years. The first major discovery here was the main Roman road from the southwest at a crucial point where it approached the crossing over the Ouse. Alongside the road were uncovered the remains of a substantial stone building which had had a long and chequered history from the mid-second to the fifth century, presenting, in many ways, a microcosm of the history of the *colonia* itself. At much the same time, part of a massive public building emerged at the Queen's Hotel site in another previously unexplored area of the Roman town near Ouse Bridge on Micklegate. One stretch of wall here survived standing to a height of 4 m (13 ft), making it one of York's most impressive archaeological finds and a foretaste of what may be found in future investigations.

We will have occasion to return to the sites just referred to, and indeed to look at many others in the following chapters. I should conclude this chapter, however, by saying that, although the pace of discovery in Roman York has accelerated markedly in the last twenty years, this is a bad time as well as a good time to write a new book on the subject. It is a good time because public and academic interest has probably never been greater, but it is a bad time, firstly, because even now no more than a minute proportion of the area occupied in Roman times has been subject to systematic archaeological excavation and, secondly, because research on most of the major sites of recent years is still in progress. It could be argued, therefore, that we know so little about Roman York, in terms of its history and layout, and the life of its people that any attempt to discuss these themes in an authoritative manner is futile. Research cannot, however, proceed by throwing up one's hands in despair and simply saying we need more data. On the contrary, I believe that by the careful analysis of what is, in spite of its many inadequacies, a large and growing body of archaeological discoveries it is possible to present a respectable account of the character and development of *Eboracum* as well as some speculation which is not entirely unfounded. My most sincere hope in presenting what follows, however, is that it will form a useful basis for further investigation of one of Britain's most remarkable Roman sites.

2
The first fortress

Setting the scene

When Quintus Petilius Cerialis, commander of the ninth legion, pitched his tent in AD 71 at what was to become *Eboracum*, he must have felt remote from the civilized world. Not only was he on an island beyond the great and terrible ocean, but he was also a long way from the fledgling province, now some 25 years old, in the south of Britain where a semblance of a Romanized way of life had been adopted by at least the more ambitious members of the community. Its location, however, at the edge of empire, renders York of particular interest to archaeologists. This is because it allows a clear view of the Roman approach to conquest and government during virtually the last gasp of that great surge out of the Italian peninsula which had brought uninterrupted military victory over the previous 200 years or so.

When Vespasian became emperor in 69 the Roman province of *Britannia* had reached a line running roughly from the Humber to the Mersey, although north Wales was not finally pacified for another ten years. Northern England as far as the Scottish lowlands was largely occupied by a people known to the Romans as the Brigantes. Rather than being a unified nation in any familiar sense, however, they were probably little more than a loose confederation linked by dynastic ties. The Brigantian population was scattered in isolated farmsteads and small villages, and there were few communal centres comparable to those which the Romans had encountered in southern England, except for a site at Stanwick, near Richmond in North Yorkshire, which was a defended enclosure covering an area of some 300 ha (741 acres). Excavations by Sir Mortimer Wheeler in the 1950s and by Durham University

in more recent times have produced Roman pottery and other artefacts such as glass which date from as early as the mid-first century. The implication of these finds is that Stanwick was the seat of a branch of the Brigantian aristocracy which had come under the influence of Roman civilization and eagerly sought its material benefits.

Our knowledge of the occasion, or pretext, for the Roman attack on Brigantia comes from the writings of the Roman author Tacitus who refers to a conflict between two parties in the Brigantian royal house which threatened the stability of the province to the south. On one side was Queen Cartimandua, who favoured good relations with the Romans, and on the other was her estranged husband Venutius who led an anti-Roman party. Trouble had been brewing since as early as 51 when Cartimandua had handed over to the Romans the fugitive rebel leader from Wales, Caratacus. Subsequently, matters were made worse when the queen took Venutius' armour-bearer, Vellocatus, as a lover. The outbreak of civil strife led to a Roman intervention and 'at the cost of desperate fighting' Cartimandua was rescued from Venutius' forces. Venutius himself had then to be dealt with and Wheeler suggested that he made a last stand at Stanwick.

Whether there is any truth in Wheeler's theory or not, one reason for the choice of York as a fortress site must have been that it was ideally placed to allow the army to strike at centres of Brigantian resistance in the valleys of the Pennines and the Yorkshire Moors. The site may also have had the advantage of lying on the boundary between the Brigantes and another native people, the Parisi, who occupied an area roughly comparable to the old East

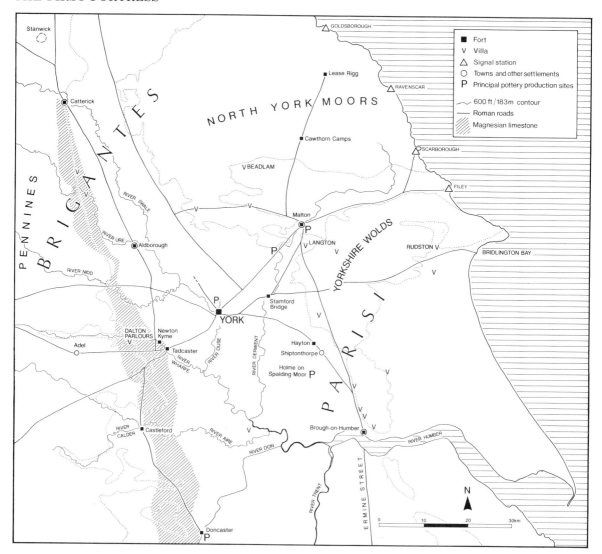

4 *Roman Yorkshire showing principal military sites, towns, villas, other settlements and pottery production centres.*

Riding of Yorkshire. In other words York was, perhaps, in a neutral zone from where both peoples could be supervised, but not unduly provoked. Nothing is known of the attitude of the Parisi to the Roman conquest, but there is no suggestion that they were hostile.

Another advantage of the York site was that it allowed good communications with the Roman province to the south. Land routes could easily be established to link York by road to Lincoln, where the ninth legion had been based before moving north, and to Chester, where a fortress was established in 78. Ships bringing men and supplies were able to come from the North Sea to the river Ouse by way of the Humber estuary. Finally, and as important as any other consideration, the Vale of York had, as it has today, some of the best agricultural land in northern England from which provisions could be found to feed over 5000 hungry soldiers.

As far as the immediate locality was concerned, York shows that the Roman military surveyors had an unerring talent for assessing a site's potential. The fortress is not only at the junction of two rivers, the Ouse and the Foss, which offered a natural defence on two sides, but it also lies on a substantial natural causeway formed by a moraine, an area of rocky debris left by retreating glaciers, which runs east-west across the low-lying, and, in places, marshy, Vale of York. The course of the rivers in Roman times is not altogether certain, but the Ouse has probably not changed a great deal over the centuries. The Foss was substantially altered by the creation of the King's Fish Pool in the eleventh century and by canalization in more recent times. It is difficult to determine the level of the rivers in the Roman period especially as they were subject to a strong tidal influence which in modern times has been restricted by Naburn lock, downstream from York. Recent small-scale excavations on the south-west bank of the Ouse suggest, however, that in the late first century its level may have been, on average, some 3–4 m (10–13 ft) below its present summer average of c.5 m (16 ft) OD. One effect of this would have been to make the slightly elevated position of the fortress much more apparent than it is today. River scouring on the north-east bank would, moreover, have created a low cliff below the fortress (see **39**), but while this would have caused problems of a sharp ascent to the main fortress gateway (*porta principalis*), it would also have had the advantage of preventing easy attack from the river. On the south-west bank of the Ouse opposite the fortress, in the area which was to become the principal civilian settlement (see Chapter 4), there was probably a gently shelving foreshore suitable for drawing up ships. Behind this the land was level for c. 100 m (330 ft), but then rose fairly sharply before levelling out again.

It appears that there was no permanent native settlement in what is now the city's historic core when the Romans arrived and the legion probably encountered a pleasant meadowland scene not unlike that on the rural reaches of the Ouse today. Research on the well-preserved organic material, including plant remains and snail shells, from recent excavations suggests a mixture of woodland scrub and cleared agricultural land. Sites close to the south-west bank of the Ouse have, as one would expect, produced the remains of organisms which are usually found in marshes, ponds and on river banks. Many of the wetland plant species recorded are rather low-growing which may indicate that the land was used for grazing by native farmers. On the north-east side of the fortress, however, it is likely that thick woodland was not far distant since we know

that in medieval times what was then called the Forest of Galtres came to within a few miles of the city walls.

In the area around York aerial photography has identified numerous traces of pre-Roman villages and farmsteads, many of which were probably occupied in the second half of the first century. One of these sites, at Naburn, some 5 km (3 miles) south of the city centre (**5-6**), has been examined in detail by Dr R. F. J. Jones of Bradford University. The remains of a number of round houses located within rectangular enclosures have been excavated (sites A, B and D) which are dated to the late pre-Roman Iron Age, but do not seem to have survived into the Roman period itself. There is evidence that the field system remained in use from the pre- to the post-conquest period. Details of agricultural practices at Naburn are scarce, as animal bone and other organic materials do not survive in the acid ground, although a charred grain deposit provided evidence for the cultivation of barley and bread-wheat. In the upland regions of Brigantian territory a greater emphasis on pastoralism is likely and Sir Mortimer Wheeler had a theory that Cartimandua was a princess of southern origin whose temper was soured by a continual diet of mutton!

The fortress and its men
In the late first century the Roman army in Britain consisted of two sorts of troops: firstly, there were three legions, each of which was made up of some 5000 men; and secondly there were the auxiliary regiments, native troops from various parts of the empire, some infantry and some mounted, in units 500 and 1000 strong. The legionaries were accommodated in fortresses, and eleven of full size are now known in Britain. Of these, York, Caerleon and Chester became permanent bases for the provincial garrison. The auxiliaries were largely based in forts, smaller establishments, of which there are many examples up and down the country. Their layout is closely comparable to that of the fortresses, albeit on a smaller scale. (For the principal components of the York fortress plan see **8**.)

The principal function of a Roman fortress was to provide accommodation for the men and equipment of a legion. Although it had defences to prevent sudden attacks by hostile forces, a fortress was not primarily designed for defence,

5 *Aerial view of the late Iron Age/Roman settlement at Lingcroft Farm, Naburn showing the enclosure in Site A.*

like a medieval castle, but was a base from which the army would go out to fight in the field. By the late first century fortresses had acquired a fairly standardized form of a playing-card-shaped enclosure of some 20 ha (50 acres) with internal buildings and streets in fixed locations. As far as Britain is concerned, one of the more extensively excavated fortresses is Inchtuthil, built in 83 on the banks of the Tay near Perth. Enough of the site has been examined to allow the broad outlines of its plan to be reconstructed and this serves as a good model against which to compare the evidence from York.

The organization of a late first-century Roman legion may be briefly summarized. The basic unit was the *contubernium* of eight men who shared a tent when on campaign and a pair of rooms in a fortress barrack. Ten *contubernia* made a century (80 men) and they were commanded by a centurion. Six centuries made up a cohort (480 men) and ten cohorts a legion. In the late first century, however, the first cohort was of double strength (960 men) and it probably included the *immunes* who were excused from fighting, but worked as administrators, priests and such specialists as surveyors, engineers and weapon smiths.

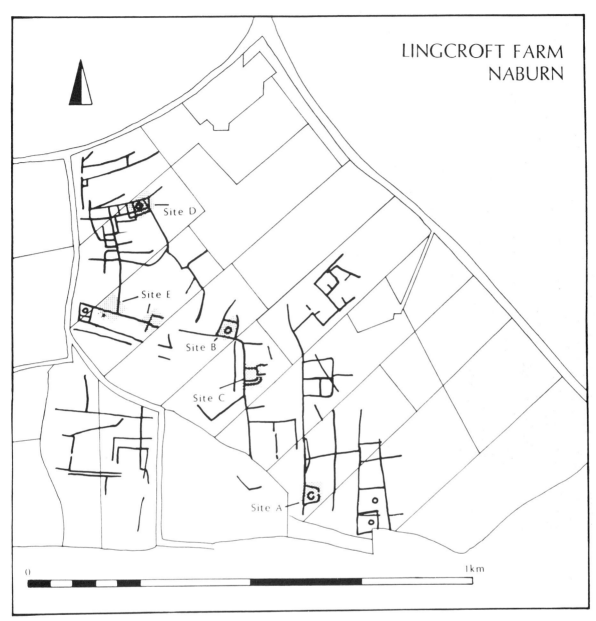

6 *Lingcroft Farm, Naburn: plan showing excavation sites and landscape features identified from aerial photographs.*

The command structure of a legion was closely integrated within the imperial social hierarchy. All legionaries were, of course, Roman citizens with access to the privileges that status conferred. In the first century the vast majority of the population of the empire were non-citizens or slaves who were subject to its laws while the citizens were protected by them. This meant, for example, that citizens had more secure rights to own and inherit property than non-citizens, and in the event of wrongdoing citizens could usually avoid the more humiliating punishments such as service in the mines or confronting wild beasts in the amphitheatre. The citizen body was, however, by no means homogeneous; some members were a good deal more privileged than others. Admission to the various social strata was nominally based on a property and wealth qualification, although there was a strong hereditary element. The post of commander of the legion, the *legatus* (legate), was reserved for a man of senatorial rank, the highest in the empire. He was probably a man in his thirties and would have been destined for the highest offices. The second-in-command, known as the *tribunus laticlavius*, would also have been of senatorial rank, but in his early twenties. The other five senior officers, the *tribuni angusticlavii*, were of the next rank down from the senators, known as equestrians or Roman knights. The equestrian tribunes would have been slightly older than the second-in-command, but again had a wide range of careers in senior military or administrative posts open to them. These senior officers usually served for only three years before moving on, but the highest-ranking officer in a more permanent post was the camp prefect (*praefectus castrorum*) who took charge of camp organization, training and equipment. The camp prefect was supported by the centurions who formed the backbone of the army's command structure.

By the late first century soldiers signed on for 25 years of service. Although this might seem unduly long, a career as a legionary was much sought after as it was seen as a route to social advancement. Legionaries not only had a steady income, but as veterans were usually given a handsome golden handshake which might include land attached to one of the *coloniae*; wealth in the form of land was the key to entering the governing classes. Retired legionaries were also allowed to marry. This does not mean that they led celibate lives while in service, however, and unofficial arrangements were doubtless made for lady-friends and families to live in civilian settlements adjacent to a fortress.

Soldiers were among those members of Roman society who had the funds and inclination to make commemorative dedications to the gods or to the memory of their deceased fellows by erecting inscribed stone monuments. We can, therefore, learn something of the soldiers in York from their altars, tombstones or coffins. Of the two tombstones which refer to men of the ninth, one is incomplete so the soldier's name is unknown, but we do know that he came from Novaria in northern Italy and that his freedmen heirs set up the stone for a 'well-deserving patron'. These freedmen were probably the man's slaves given their liberty, or manumission, under the terms of his will and so we have an insight here into the personal wealth that some legionaries could command. The second ninth legion tombstone is one of the finest from York and was erected for the standard bearer (*signifer*) Lucius Duccius Rufinus (**colour plate 1**). He is shown holding a standard in his right hand and a case of writing tablets in his left which may represent his will. The inscription tells us that Rufinus hailed from *Vienna* (Vienne) in the Rhône valley in south-east Gaul and this serves to make the point that the men who came to York with both the ninth and sixth legions had diverse geographical origins. Whereas Julius Caesar's troops in the mid-first century BC came largely from Italy, Rufinus is typical of the recruits from the Gallic provinces who were entering the army in large numbers in the late first century AD.

Another ninth legion inscription from York is to be found on an altar set up by the clerk (*cornicularius*), Celerinius Vitalis to Silvanus, a god of the woods. This seems an eminently appropriate dedication for a member of a legion that was campaigning in the wild and mysterious country of the north, but whose favourite pastime was hunting wild boar and other game.

The layout of the fortress

With an outline of the structure of a legion in mind, we may turn now to the layout of the fortress at York. Although its corners were close to the cardinal points, this is unlikely to have had any particular significance and a more important consideration in setting out the site is likely to have been to get it as level as possible. It has become clear from excavations, however, that ground level within the fortress was at its highest in the centre and the western quadrant, but sloped down towards the east corner, and more markedly, towards the south corner. At the Minster natural ground level occurs at *c*.13.5 m (44 ft) OD and at Interval Tower SW5 *c*.14 m (46 ft) OD, but near the east corner at 7–9 Aldwark the natural level was found at *c*.12 m (39 ft) OD while at 16 Parliament Street it is at *c*.11 m (36 ft) OD.

Once the site had been chosen, we may be certain that the fortress was carefully laid out and the legionary surveyors (*agrimensores*) probably had a manual giving details of how this was to be done. Because of both the presence of a modern city on the site and continuous occupation and redesign during the Roman period itself, very little detail of York's original first-century plan is known. By the late first century, however, British fortresses had become so standardized that once a little is known about a site, including the line of its defences and its principal streets, and the location of some of the more important buildings, the rest of the plan can be determined with some degree of confidence. This has been made easier by the discovery at Colchester, and subsequently Exeter and elsewhere, that Britain's fortresses were laid out on the basis of units of the Roman foot or *pes Monetalis* (1pM = 0.296 m or 0.97 imperial feet), so-called after the standard to be found in the temple of Juno Moneta in Rome.

The Roman surveyor's principal instrument was the *groma* (7), which consisted of an iron cross with four arms at 90 degrees to one another, each of which had a plumb line suspended from the end. Another line hung from the centre of the cross so that it could be set over a fixed point. The instrument was supported on a staff which was positioned off-centre to enable the surveyor to sight through opposing plumb lines and, with the aid of ranging poles, survey straight lines and right angles. For the purposes of measuring, the surveyors had rules for shorter distances, and rods and chains for longer.

The main problem with using a *groma* was to keep the plumb lines still in windy conditions, but otherwise it appears that the Romans were able to survey with a reasonable degree of accuracy. Discrepancies still do appear in fortress plans, usually fairly minor, between the actual measurements on the ground and what we believe was the original blueprint. These may be due, on the one hand, to the inadequacies of the surveying equipment or to adjustments to localized topographical problems. On the other hand, archaeologists may themselves introduce inaccuracies where none actually existed because they often work with plans at a relatively small scale. Furthermore, modern surveying, especially on confined and enclosed archaeological sites, is far from error free. None of these problems, however, obscures the evidence for regularity, based on units of the Roman foot, in the plans of many Roman military sites including the fortress at York.

7 *The* groma *in use.*

There are three principal reasons for studying the measurements of Roman sites. Firstly, it is of interest to know how fortresses, towns and so forth were surveyed and laid out. Secondly, it may be possible to classify metrological schemes which can be tied to particular periods or, in the case of forts and fortresses, to particular army units. Thirdly, metrology imposes a discipline on both the interpretation of what may, as at York, be very fragmentary remains and on the planning of future archaeological work. The measurements given below, which have been used for a theoretical reconstruction of the late first-century plan of the York fortress (see **8** and **9**), are based on the most accurate 1:1250 plan available and, where possible, on larger-scale plans of archaeological excavations.

The first task for the legionary surveyors was to decide the orientation of the headquarters building, or *principia*, which in turn determined the orientation of the fortress itself. At York the fortress faces south-west towards the river Ouse. That part of the fortress which lay in front of the *principia* was known as the *praetentura*, the areas on either side of the *principia* were known as the *latera praetorii*, and the part behind the *principia* was known as the *retentura*.

In order to understand how the fortress was laid out it may be divided into two distinct, if related, elements: firstly, the interior space used for buildings and streets and, secondly, the defensive envelope consisting, in the first century, of a rampart and ditch. Having decided on orientation, the surveyor's next task was probably to mark out the line enclosing the interior space and dividing it from the defences (**9a**). The work was set in train by placing the *groma* at the intended intersection of the two main streets, the *via principalis* which ran in front of the headquarters building to join the two side gates, and the *via praetoria* which ran to the main gate or *porta praetoria*. By analogy with discoveries elsewhere it is quite likely that votive offerings were buried at the intersection of the main streets to invite the gods to look favourably on the fortress and its future occupants.

At York the intended dimensions of the space within the defences of the late first-century fortress appear to have been 1600 pM (473.6 m/ 1554 ft) north-east/south-west by 1360 pM (402.56 m/1321 ft) north-west/south-east. The only deviation from a true rectangle may have occurred at the north-east corner where the south-east defences appear to have run slightly off a straight line. These dimensions were probably chosen for two reasons: firstly, they would provide sufficient space to accommodate the legion in a tried and tested manner; and, secondly, the measurements allowed for easy setting-out and internal subdivision without the need for complex measuring and surveying exercises. While the surveyors who designed the plan were highly-trained specialists, the legionaries are unlikely to have had numeracy skills of a consistently high order. They therefore had to have a plan which could be easily realized and checked for accuracy.

The choice of a length of 1600 pM is related to an internal division into a *praetentura* measuring 700 pM (207.2 m/680 ft) north-east/south-west, a *principia* and *latera praetorii* measuring 300 pM (88.8 m/288 ft), and a *retentura* measuring 600 pM (177.6 m/583 ft). The *praetentura* was then subdivided into three strips (1–3), one 300 pM (88.8 m/289 ft) wide and two 200 pM (59.2 m/194 ft) wide. The *retentura* was subdivided into two strips (5–6) each 300 pM wide.

A width north-west/south-east of 1360 pM was probably combined with a length of 1600 pM to make it easy to ensure that the

8 *The Roman fortress at York showing the principal components of the plan and location of archaeological sites referred to in the text. (The designation of the stone interval towers follows that of the Royal Commission on Historical Monuments).*

1 Porta decumana: intervallum *building*
2 *Aldwark 1971–72: Interval Tower NE6 and rampart*
3 *Aldwark 1971–72: rampart*
4 *East corner: defences*
5 *7–9 Aldwark: defences*
6 *1–5 Aldwark: barracks*
7 *Bedern Trench 1: barracks*
8 *Treasurer's House: via decumana*
9 *Hawarden Place: defences*
10 *Bedern Trench 5: unidentified buildings*
11 *Bedern Trench 3/4: defences and unidentified buildings*
12 *Dean's Park: intervallum buildings and defences*
13 *Purey Cust nursing home: first cohort barracks*
14 *Minster excavations: first cohort barracks*
15 *Minster excavations: principia*
16 *Low Petergate: unidentified buildings*
17 *Bootham Bar: porta principalis dextra and fortress wall*
18 *Exhibition Square: fortress wall and interval tower*
19 *9 Blake Street (Former City Garage, now Stonegate Walk): unidentified buildings.*
20 *Back Swinegate: baths*
21 *Church Street: sewer and baths*
22 *Church Street watching brief: intervallum*
23 *Roman Bath public house: baths*
24 *'Anglian' Tower*
25 *Defences between the 'Anglian' Tower and the Multangular Tower*
26 *Davygate: barracks and defences*
27 *Parliament Street sewer trench: fortress wall*
28 *16 Parliament Street: defences*
29 *Interval Tower SW5: defences*
30 *Judge's Lodgings: intervallum building*
31 *8 (formerly 50–1) Coney Street: defences*

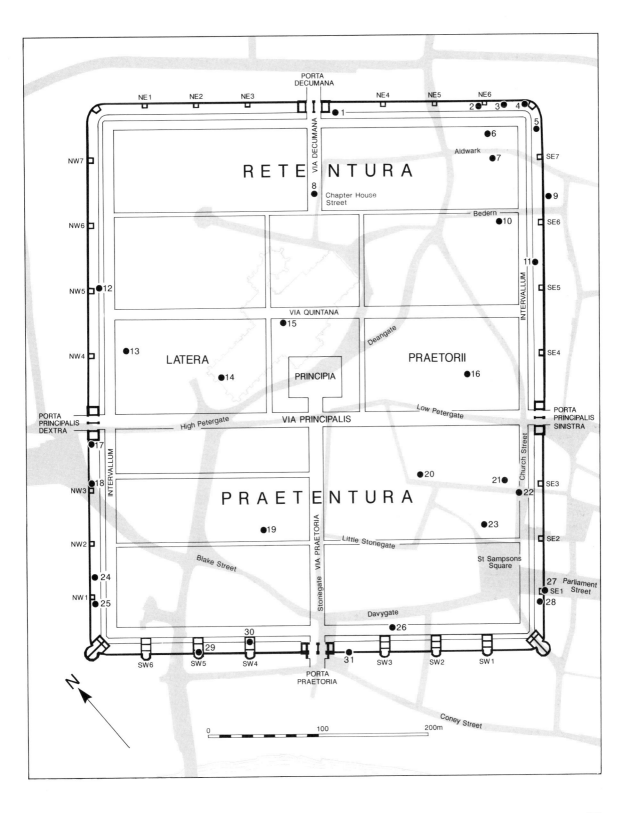

corners of the site were at 90 degrees. Creating right-angled corners is one of the biggest problems in surveying a large and somewhat uneven site with simple instruments. If the site was 1600×1360 pM, however, the diagonal across the site was exactly 2100 pM (621.6 m/2039 ft), a good round number which could easily be checked during laying out to ensure that the sides were parallel. 2100 was also 60×35 pM (10.36 m/34 ft) and, as we will see, a 35 pM unit was frequently employed elsewhere in the fortress plan.

Once the six strips had been laid out, the next step was to lay out the principal street spaces (9b). The *via principalis* which, as at Inchtuthil, was probably 60 pM (17.76 m/58 ft) wide was taken from the north-east side of Strip 3. By analogy with Inchtuthil and other fortresses of this period, it is likely that space for a portico was taken from each side of the street. Some evidence for this feature was found in the Minster excavations and it was probably 10 pM (2.96 m/10 ft) wide, leaving a central carriageway 40 pM (11.84 m/39 ft) wide. The spaces for the *via praetoria* and its continuation to the rear of the *principia*, the *via decumana*, were probably 60 pM wide, again with porticoes 10 pM wide on each side. Evidence for a portico fronted by stone columns was found on the south-east side of the *via decumana* in an excavation at the Treasurer's House. It is not known, however, if the columns had replaced an earlier timber portico and they may represent a reconstruction of the second century. There are few records of the *via praetoria*, which is not surprising as much of it lies underneath modern Stonegate, but it seems to have had a central gutter while below it was a stone-built sewer.

Around the perimeter of the fortress site, behind the defences, ran a space known as the *intervallum* (see 8). This served to lessen the chance of any enemy missiles which cleared the defences damaging buildings. It also accommodated a street known as the *via sagularis* which allowed troops to be moved quickly around the fortress to any point of attack. At York the *intervallum* is known from the excavation of Bedern Trench 3/4, near the east corner, to have been 35 pM wide in the late first century, although it was widened in the second century. Spaces planned for streets, other than the main ones, were not always surfaced, it may be noted that no late first-century *via*

sagularis was found in the Bedern trench, although an early gravel surface was seen in a watching brief at Church Street in the *praetentura*.

The next stage in fortress layout was the addition of the minor street spaces. Working from the south-west, the first street was probably taken from the south-west side of Strip 2. This was located at 9 Blake Street where it was 10 pM (2.96 m/10 ft) wide, but again was not surfaced in the late first century. The next street, which has not yet been recorded, was, on metrological grounds, probably taken from the south-west side of Strip 3, but it cannot have run the whole distance from the *via praetoria* to the south-east *intervallum* because of the baths block (see pp. 31–3). The *via quintana* (literally the fifth street), which is the street running north-west/south-east behind the *principia*, was recorded in the Minster excavations; it was probably 35 pM wide and was taken out of the north-east side of Strip 4. The street space between Strips 5 and 6 has not been uncovered, although its location can be confidently predicted. No minor street spaces running north-east/south-west have been discovered except for that north-west of the *principia* which in excavation was found to be 35 pM wide. It can be presumed that the space to the south-east was also 35 pM wide.

Once this basic framework had been established, work could start on the construction of buildings. At the centre was the headquarters building (for the plan see 22) where the administration of the legion took place and official religious ceremonies were observed. It would have consisted of a courtyard surrounded on three sides by a colonnaded portico and on the fourth by an aisled hall, or basilica. This would have been a lofty structure, perhaps as much as 20 m (65 ft) high. At one or both ends there would have been a raised podium from which the commanding officer could address his troops.

At the back of the basilica there would

9 *A theoretical reconstruction of the late first-century fortress plan showing the principal measurements in Roman feet.*
P = principia
B = bath house

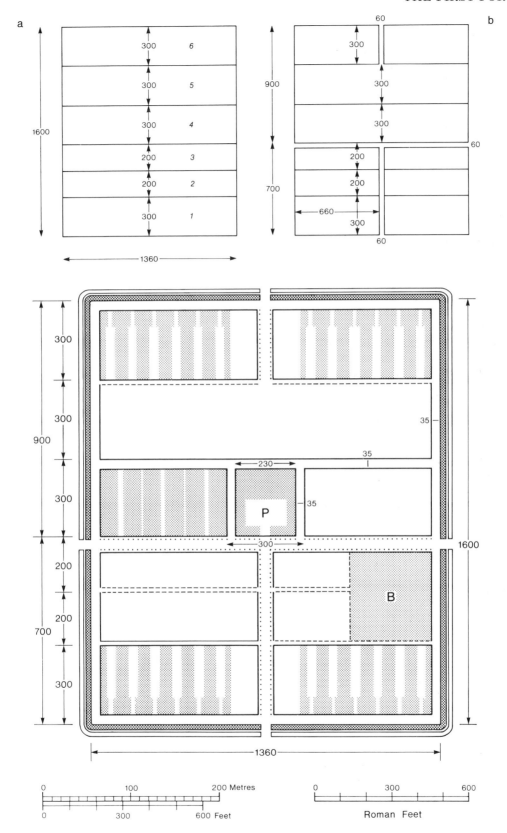

have been a row of rooms, usually five in number. They served as offices except for the one in the centre which was the *aedes*, the legionary shrine, in which sacred cult statues were kept along with the legion's standards when the men were not out on campaign. Below the *aedes* there was probably a cellar used as a strongroom for legion funds and the soldiers' pay and savings.

At York the remains discovered at the Minster were of a stone building dating to *c*.100, which probably replaced a timber structure whose plan is unknown. Although only parts of the basilica and offices were excavated, it is clear that the space for the headquarters building (excluding exterior porticoes) was planned to be $265 \times 230\,\text{pM}$ ($78.44\,\text{m} \times 68.08\,\text{m}/257\,\text{ft} \times 223\,\text{ft}$). One reason for choosing these particular measurements may, again, be to do with ensuring the corners had 90 degree angles as the diagonal across the plot is almost exactly $350\,\text{pM}$ ($103.6\,\text{m}/340\,\text{ft}$) an easily checkable figure: 350 is also $10 \times 35\,\text{pM}$ or $\frac{1}{6}$ of the diagonal of the internal space of the fortress. Around the outside of the headquarters building on all but the north-east side there was a covered portico. As already noted, its width was probably $10\,\text{pM}$ on the south-west, but on the north-west and presumably on the south-east side it was $17.5\,\text{pM}$ (i.e. half of $35\,\text{pM}$ and $c.5.2\,\text{m}/17\,\text{ft}$) wide.

Religion in the fortress

The importance of the legionary shrine as both the physical and emotional focus of the fortress cannot be overstated. Roman religion was characterized firstly by its diversity, with innumerable deities, some local, some empire-wide, receiving devotion, and secondly by its pervasive influence on every aspect of life in a way which we would probably find totally alien today. The contrast between then and now must, to some extent, be a product of the greater control over our destiny that we believe material prosperity and scientific knowledge have given us. In Roman times people were often faced with economic forces over which they had little influence and they also lived with the constant hazards of war and incurable disease. In such circumstances it is no surprise that they felt a much more urgent need to propitiate any supernatural forces which might ensure a secure and prosperous future. This idea of making a bargain with the gods was

given ritual form in sacrifices and offerings, and the associated ceremonies lie at the heart of all Roman worship.

It is also worth stressing that the Roman world, in spite of its great cities, was overwhelmingly agrarian and for both Romans and natives the fortunes of agriculture were of paramount importance. As a result the timetable of religious practice throughout the empire was closely linked with the cycle of the seasons and revolved around a concern for the continuing fertility of beasts and crops. A community of interests between Roman and native in these matters goes a long way towards explaining the frequent merging of classical and native deities which brought about new hybrids with attributes and powers drawn from both traditions.

Religion in Roman Britain may be divided up into cults which were officially sponsored and those which were practised unofficially on a day-to-day basis. In observance of official religion the statues in the fortress shrine would probably have included representations of the three principal deities in the Roman pantheon, Jupiter, Juno and Minerva, often known as the Capitoline Triad because of their temples on the Capitoline Hill in Rome. The members of triad were particularly associated with the well-being and security of the empire and dedications to them are common in Britain, especially in military areas, although there is only one from York. This appears on the Bishophill altar, where Jupiter is combined with the gods and goddesses of hospitality and home by the dedicator, one Publius Aelius Marcianus, the commander of a body of auxiliary troops.

In addition to representations of the Capitoline Triad, the legionary shrine probably contained an image of the emperor. As chief priest (*pontifex maximus* as Trajan is described on the King's Square inscription), he would have dominated the sacred as well as the secular life of the empire. Strictly speaking, emperors were not treated as gods while living, but might be deified after their deaths. The living emperor's spirit (his *numen*) was, however, considered to have sacred power and dedications were made to it by soldiers and civilians alike. In a sense, the cult of the emperor was Roman ancestor worship on a grand scale, the emperor being conceived as father of his people, but it was energetically promoted by the state because it provided a unifying spiritual and emotional focus for the disparate subject people who might otherwise have little in common.

Attendance at the official ceremonies honouring the Capitoline Triad and deified emperors would have been compulsory for the soldiers, and a team of priests and augurs (*haruspices*) was carried on the legion's strength, but otherwise the men were free to indulge in whatever religious practices they chose. It is, therefore, characteristic of forts and fortresses that they were surrounded by diverse temples and altars, and at York there is some evidence for a concentration on the south-east side (see p.69). Deities favoured by soldiers would have included those in the classical pantheon, such as Mars and Hercules, who presided over war and combat, and those created as personifications of martial qualities, such as *Victoria* (victory) and *Fortuna* (fortune). The men would also have worshipped deities of their homelands, of countries in which they had seen service and of the locality in which they presently found themselves, often personified as the *Genius Loci* (spirit of the place).

Other buildings in the fortress
Returning now to the plan of the fortress we move across the *via quintana* from the headquarters basilica. This probably brings us to the commanding officer's house (*praetorium*), the south-west corner of which was seen in the Minster excavations. This may be envisaged as something of an island of domestic tranquillity in the bustling military world and would have approximated in plan and appointments to the luxurious town houses of the period, with a central courtyard and garden surrounded by ranges of rooms.

Other major buildings in the fortress would have included granaries, workshops and a hospital, but at York the only other facility about which anything is known is the bath house. Baths were a vital part of Roman life not only for washing, but also for a range of social activities; in modern municipal parlance they functioned as a 'leisure centre'. As a result, baths needed a large area, so large in fact that fort bath houses were usually outside the defences and only fortresses had sufficient space within them. At York the bath house plot was located on the south-east side of the *praetentura*, and occupied c.9100 sq.m (10,900 sq. yds).

Because they needed heat and water, bath houses had to be constructed largely of stone while other fortress buildings could use timber. The presence of a late first-century stone building has recently been demonstrated at the Back Swinegate site, although no details of its plan are evident. The most spectacular discovery in the fortress baths at York, however, was the main sewer located on the north side of Church Street (**10**). The principal channel, fed by a number of side channels, was found running for some 44 m (144 ft) on a north-west/south-east line to a point close to the edge of the *intervallum* where it returned to the north-east.

The sewer was constructed from massive blocks of millstone grit and limestone, and was almost large enough for a person of average height to stand up in. In places there were round arches which presumably supported walls in the building above. The sewer's function was to remove water and other waste from the baths and latrines, and its size indicates the vast quantity of water that was used when the place was going full blast. At Exeter it has been calculated that the legionary baths may have used some 318,000 litres (70,000 gallons) a day. The source of the water used at York is difficult to determine; it may have been pumped out of the rivers Foss and Ouse, but another source was suggested by examination of the silt deposits in the sewer which, surprisingly, produced the seeds and pollen of plants which prefer limestone subsoil. This suggests the existence of an aqueduct to bring water from the nearest limestone country, probably in the Tadcaster area some 20 km (12 miles) away to the south-west or in the North York Moors to the north-east, but no trace of it has ever been found. We should not necessarily, however, be thinking in terms of a massive stone structure like the well-known aqueducts in the Mediterranean world which had to cross great valleys and gorges. Where known, aqueducts in Britain were mostly large ditches which followed the line of natural contours, the water being channelled through some kind of ceramic or concrete pipe.

The usual practice before bathing in Roman style was to work up a sweat with exercise and then to enter the hot room, or *caldarium* where the sweat and dirt were removed with a form of scraper known as a *strigil*. The *caldarium* was heated by hot air circulating below a floor raised on pillars (*pilae*) and might also be sent up the walls in hollow flue tiles. Part of the

10 *Peter Addyman (Director of York Archaeological Trust) inspects the main channel of the
Roman sewer which served the legionary
fortress baths at the Church Street site, 1972.*

York fortress *caldarium* was excavated in 1930
and an apsed end wall and large millstone grit
blocks which originally supported the floor can
still be seen in the public house called the
Roman Bath. A heated room was also found on
the Church Street site where the floors had

been supported on pillars of tile (**11**). Other
rooms in the baths, the location of which is not
known at York, would have included a hot
room to provide the dry heat of a sauna and a
frigidarium with a cold plunge to close the
skin's pores after bathing.

Finds of bone and pottery counters from
the silt in the sewer suggest that, aside from
bathing, a popular activity in the baths was
the playing of, and doubtless gambling on,
board games such as *ludus duodecim scrip-
torum*, a form of backgammon, and *ludus latrun-*

11 *Church Street: a heated room with tile* pilae *in the fortress baths.*

culorum, a form of chess. Personal items found included two gold pendants (**colour plate 4**) which had probably been worn as amulets or charms, and a number of intaglios, the carved gemstones used in seal rings, with representations of Mars, Roma and Fortuna, deities appropriate to the soldier and his world (**12**).

More robust entertainments than those poss-ible in the baths would have been on offer in the amphitheatre, and a slip of bone bearing the inscription DOMINE VICTOR VINCAS FELIX ('Lord Victor may you have a lucky win') found in a Roman coffin hints that gladiators practised their bloodthirsty skills in York. As yet no amphitheatre has been found at York, but by a process of elimination it may be suggested that it lay to the south-east of the fortress (see 1, 5). On some of the early maps of York, more-over, the line of the streets Aldwark and Hun-gate, which are probably Anglo-Scandinavian or earlier in origin, suggests that they had been laid out to avoid the remains of a large structure with an elliptical plan. This may indicate that the amphitheatre was sited between St Andrewgate and St Saviourgate.

This survey of the buildings of the early fortress can be concluded with a brief look at the soldiers' living accommodation. Excavations at 9 Blake Street, in the *praetentura*, revealed the remains of what may have been a self-contained residential block (**13**) and it is possible that it formed one of the Tribune's houses, although in other fortresses they usually faced the *via principalis*.

Overlying a number of pits and gullies which must relate to the earliest Roman presence at York, before the fortress had been built, there were two episodes of timber building at 9 Blake Street: one late first century and the second a reconstruction of, perhaps, the early second. The buildings were identified from a series of slots 20–40 cm (8–16 in) wide and 20–25 cm (8–10 in) deep. These had once held timber beams into which uprights were morticed at intervals. By analogy with fortress buildings elsewhere, the walls between the uprights were probably made of wattles, trimmed wooden rods, which were plastered with clay, or daub as it is usually known. No timber survived on the site and it had probably been carefully removed when the buildings were rebuilt in stone in the second century (see p.55). The building plan consisted of two ranges of rooms on a north-west/south-east alignment separated by a small alley. As will become clearer when we look at the stone buildings, the north-eastern range probably contained living quarters and the south-western a service range identified primarily by the presence of hearths, presumably for cooking. A remarkable component of the finds associated with the timber buildings was a large number of pottery lamps (**14**) which came from a restricted area immediately to the north-west of the residential range. Lamps were often used in religious ritual and so there may have been some sort of shrine in the vicinity.

The barracks in which the ordinary legionaries lived were located around the perimeter of the site, except for those of the first cohort, which were located north-west of the *principia*. Each barrack-block housed a century and normally consisted of 10 pairs of rooms, each pair accommodating eight men, and at the end

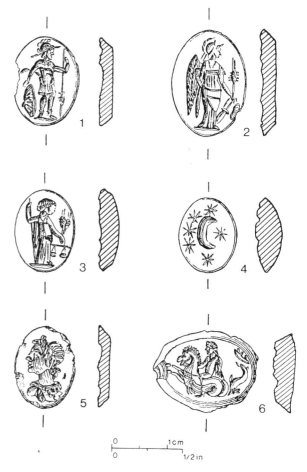

12 *Intaglios from the Church Street sewer. 1 Mars. 2 Fortuna. 3 Aequitas (equity). 4 Moon and stars symbolizing the heavens, home of Jupiter. 5 Maenad – participant in the cult of Bacchus. 6 Cupid on a hippocamp – symbolizing the soul's journey to the Isles of the Blessed.*

nearest the defences was a suite of rooms for the centurion. Very little is known of the late first-century timber barracks at York, but on the basis of the predictable nature of fortress plans it is likely that the south-west side of the *praetentura* and north-east side of the *retentura* were occupied by barrack-blocks and that they were 265 pM (*c*.78.5 m/258 ft) long. In the Aldwark/Bedern area two sites (1–5 Aldwark and Bedern Trench 5) produced beam slots and post-holes and, although fragmentary, they can be interpreted as indicating that a barrack pair, including the alley dividing it from the next

13 *Remains of timber buildings in the legionary fortress at 9 Blake Street showing beam slots and post-holes (looking south-west; 2 m scale).*

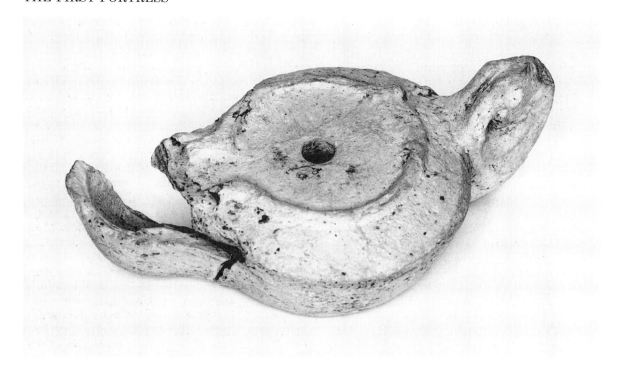

14 *Two pottery lamps from 9 Blake Street*
(length c. 70 mm (3 in)).

pair, was probably planned as 85 pM (*c*.25 m/82 ft) wide. On the basis of the Inchtuthil plan it is suggested that the barracks were organized as shown in **9**, which would mean spaces 105 pM (3 × 35) wide remained between them and the *via principalis* or *via decumana*. At Inchtuthil these spaces were occupied by small compartments known as *tabernae* which may have served as stables or store rooms. Few remains were recovered of the timber barracks of the first cohort, but if the stone versions of the mid-second century had much the same overall dimensions, then each block was about twice the width (*c*.21 m/69 ft) of the ordinary barracks. Little is known of the internal appointments of the barracks, but from excavated debris we know that the walls were plastered and given simple designs based on red stripes.

The late first-century defences

The fortress defences present us with some of Roman York's most difficult archaeological problems. Although they have been extensively studied, notably by Wellbeloved in 1840s and Miller in the 1920s, many difficulties regarding the sequence of construction remain. It is, nonetheless, my opinion that, as a result of recent work, the interpretations offered by the Royal Commission and others are now in need of radical review. In a book of this kind it is neither possible nor desirable to enter into all the reasoning behind the discussion offered in this and subsequent chapters, but three basic problems continue to complicate the analysis of the defences and they should be referred to here. Firstly, artefacts suitable for dating the various ditches, ramparts and walls are very scarce (see pp.47–50 for further discussion of the dating of Roman York). Secondly, it can be difficult to determine whether differences in structural technique indicate work in different periods or variations within a single episode of construction. Thirdly, it has become apparent that one cannot assume that a particular episode of construction work identified on one site on the defences will necessarily be matched in every detail on others. In the past there has probably been over emphasis on the search for a generalized scheme of circuit-wide changes at given periods, which has led to a good deal of special pleading for some very inadequate evidence.

In the late first century it seems likely that there was a single episode of construction involving the digging of a ditch and erection of a rampart. There are, however, no subsequent circuit-wide changes which can be dated to a single period. Some construction in stone took place early in the second century followed by further work in stone in the later second and third centuries, but it is not possible to argue convincingly for more than one phase of walling on any part of the circuit. All additions to the defences after the late first century should, instead, be seen in terms of a series of stages in a gradual remodelling, the end result of which was to emerge in the late third century.

Returning now to AD 71, we may suppose that once the overall site limits had been surveyed, work on the ditch and rampart started as a matter of priority (**15**). The ditch is the least known component of the defences and has only been fully examined in two places: Interval Towers SW5 and SW6. In both cases a complex sequence of recutting was identified, but the earliest ditch was of typical military form with sloping sides and a flat bottom. An open space, the berm, separated the ditch from the rampart behind. The line of the outer edge of the rampart was, in places at least, initially marked by a shallow trench which served to keep the construction gangs on a straight line. The men began work by placing timbers, probably oak logs, on the ground surface to create a stable base. The rampart was then built up with a core of clay and turf bands, and given a turf facing. In most of the places where the rampart has been examined further layers of timber were found, serving as strapping to bind the structure together. At the rear of the rampart the base was vertical for *c*.1 m (3¼ ft), a feature which, together with a steep slope at the rear, restricted the approach to the walkway on top. Stairs, placed at intervals around the circuit, would have allowed access.

Although it did not encounter the ditch, Bedern Trench 3/4 has provided the most comprehensive cross-section through the fortress defences in recent years. It extended *c*.30 m (98 ft) from the front of the rampart through the *intervallum* space to the buildings beyond and is, therefore, of great value for determining the relationship of the defences themselves to the interior of the fortress. As far as the earliest rampart was concerned, the trench suggests that it was *c*.6 m (19 ft) wide. It has not been possible to record the full original height at any

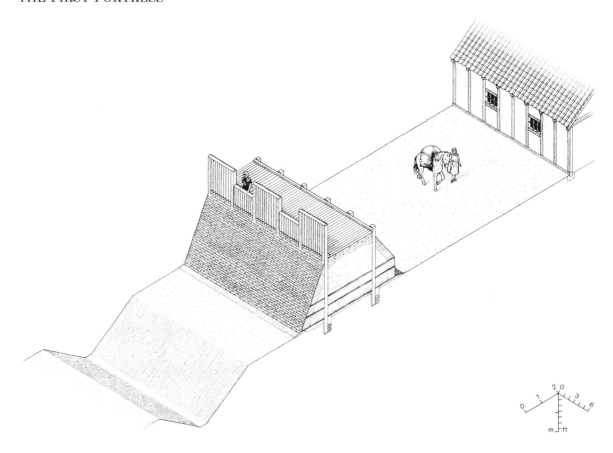

15 *A hypothetical reconstruction of the late first-century fortress defences.*

site excavated, except perhaps at the Anglian Tower where it probably stood *c*.3 m (10 ft) high. This figure is likely to be correct as it is comparable to the height of contemporary ramparts which have survived intact elsewhere. On top of the rampart there would have been a walkway *c*.2.5 m (8 ft) wide, a timber palisade and, at intervals, timber towers – post-holes for which have been found on the south-west side of the fortress at Davygate and Interval Tower SW5. The gates would also have been of timber at this stage, but nothing is known of them.

In metrological terms it seems likely that the overall width of the defensive envelope was intended to be 45 pM (13.3 m/44 ft) with the rampart 20 pM wide (5.92 m/19 ft 6 in) and the berm 10 pM (2.96 m/10 ft) wide. Based principally on the section at Interval Tower SW5 it is suggested that the ditch was intended to be 15 pM (4.44 m/15 ft) wide. We may also note that the distance north-west/south-east across the fortress ramparts was 1400 pM (1360 pM internal space plus 40 pM for ramparts) so that the *praetentura* plus rampart was divisible into two squares of 700 pM sides. Since 1400 and 700 are divisible by 35 this distinctive unit once more plays a part in the laying out of the York site.

On the basis of the location of the two timber towers Tony Sumpter, the excavator of the Interval Tower SW5 site, suggested that to achieve an even spacing there must have been ten towers on the south-west front. This was probably set out by dividing the distance of 1400 pM (414.4 m/1360 ft) across the fortress into twelve units of 110 pM (32.4 m/106 ft) with a single unit of 80 pM (23.68 m/78 ft) in the centre (**16**). From each unit a space of 11 pM, one tenth of 110, was allocated to a tower which was probably 20 pM long. It may be suggested that the 80 pM wide unit in the centre was divided into 40 pM for the carriageway of the *porta praetoria* and 20 pM for towers on either side.

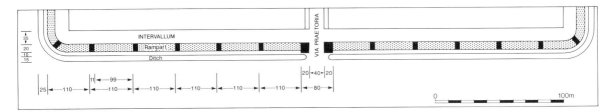

16 *The proposed metrology of the late first-century defences on the south-west side of the fortress (measurements in Roman feet).*

The legion and its roads

Although based in York, the ninth legion would have spent a good deal of its time on campaign, especially during the governorship of Agricola (78–84) when the north-west of England and much of Scotland were conquered. In addition to fighting, a vital part of the work of conquest was fort building and road construction. The Roman army's usual method of pacifying conquered territory was to establish a network of forts connected by roads; this broke up potentially hostile people into small groups and prevented them coming together as a large army. These roads are, of course, the stuff of myth and legend, especially as regards their straightness. When looked at in detail, however, Roman roads were not always as straight as we suppose, though they often incorporated long straight stretches since their main purpose was to get troops from A to B as quickly as possible. Furthermore, the military surveyors had no need to worry about routing roads around anyone's property as Roman rule was absolute.

The course of the major Roman roads in the York area is fairly well known (see **1**) and their line is often preserved in modern roads and other topographical features. One of the first roads to York followed the route believed to have been taken by the legion on its initial advance. This was a continuation of what is now known as Ermine Street, which ran north from London to Lincoln and then on to the Humber. On the north side of the Humber the road ran from a fort at Brough-on-Humber to another at Hayton near Market Weighton and then approached York from the east. Although this may have been the first Roman road to York, the most important, the Roman equiva-

lent of the A1, was that which approached from the south-west. From Tadcaster, south-west of York and known to the Romans as *Calcaria* ('limestone quarries') where there was probably a fort, the line of the Roman road corresponds closely to that of the present A64 as far as the York outskirts.

In the Dringhouses and Mount area, excavations have shown that the Roman road ran a little to the north-west of the modern Tadcaster road, although its course as it approaches the city walls is unclear. The excavations at the Wellington Row and 27 Tanner Row sites confirmed, however, that the road would have crossed the line of the city walls at Micklegate Bar where it was seen in 1910. From the Bar the road headed north-eastwards in a straight line down the valley side to the river crossing. For much of this stretch it had the still visible advantage of following a slight ridge giving natural drainage on either side. On the other side of the river the road continued on the same line through the fortress gateway and, as the *via praetoria*, ran up to the fortress headquarters.

In the excavations at Wellington Row, trenches were dug through the complete thickness of the road for the first time revealing some 4 m (13 ft) of superimposed surfaces, the latest lying just below modern ground level. We will return to these trenches again in later chapters, but at this point we must concentrate on the construction of the earliest surface which was presumably the work of the ninth legion in about 71. The earliest archaeological deposits consisted of layers of turf and a spread of hazel branches, many of them bearing nuts. At first it was thought that this material was ground preparation for the road, a way of creating a stable base on soft ground, but while the turf may have had this function the branches bear no comparison to the sturdy wattle and timberwork used as a base for Roman roads elsewhere. Instead it can be suggested that the hazel branches and a wooden bowl made from a piece of alder (**17**) found underneath them, had a religious significance and formed an offering to the local deities for the good fortune of those using the road. The hazel may have grown in one of the sacred groves so favoured by native British religion and the nuts had, perhaps, a particular significance as symbols of fruitfulness. This is, therefore, a good example of a votive foundation deposit of the kind which is common in the Roman world and, as we shall see, occurs in other contexts at York.

The first road surface was c.10 m (33 ft) wide with a camber on each side to allow drainage. The fact that the road sloped gently down towards the river suggests that the crossing was by ferry at this time. It is even possible that at low tide the river was fordable. At all events, a bridge would not have been feasible given the difference between the natural levels on the opposing river banks (see **39**). Overlying the early road surface was a deposit of clean silt, clearly deposited by water and probably the result of a flood. Although York has become well known for its floods in recent years, this is the first and only evidence for one ever found archaeologically. The Romans may have been taken by surprise by the rising waters, but their response was to build the road level up by about 1 m ($3\frac{1}{4}$ ft) with a mound (*agger*) of large cobbles which were covered by layers of finer, hard-packed gravel (**18**).

There is not sufficient space here to discuss the other Roman roads around York in detail, but it may be noted that the main road from the south-west continued beyond the fortress in a north-easterly direction towards Malton where a fort was established early in the conquest period. The road surface has been found in the area of Grove Lane which lies on the road line. Continuity from Roman times is also suggested by Bootham, which corresponds to a road to the north-west, and it is likely that Colliergate, Fossgate and Fawcett Street lie on the line of a road to the south-east.

The legion and its supplies

The arrival of the legion at York would have had a major impact on the local economy, creating a sudden increase in demand for a wide range of commodities, particularly building materials and foodstuffs. It is not entirely clear how the army went about supplying itself, but we may presume a mixture of direct requisitioning, various forms of trade, based on both barter and the use of coinage, and a certain amount of manufacturing at the fortress site. Local resources would have been most convenient, but if they were inadequate material was presumably shipped in from elsewhere.

On arrival at York the legion would have organized an area of land adjacent to the fortress (*territorium*) which it managed directly for supply purposes. The location and size of the York *territorium* is unknown, but since one of the legion's most immediate requirements in 71 was timber, it may have taken control of land to the north-east of the fortress which, as already suggested, was probably densely forested. In addition, the army needed stone, and areas suitable for quarrying may also have been included in the *territorium*. No certain Roman quarries can be located today, but two types of stone used from the late first century onwards can both be found no more than 30 km (19 miles) from York on its west side. Millstone grit, a coarse sandstone usually existing as massive blocks, was employed in monumental structures such as the sewer, where its load-bearing properties were of particular value, and it was also frequently used for sculptures, especially funerary monuments. Equally popular for both building and sculpture was the magnesian limestone from the quarries in Tadcaster. This is a high quality freestone, that is it has no distinct bedding plane and can be cut in any direction. In Roman structures it usually occurs in small blocks, and these can still be seen in surviving stretches of the fortress wall. A second type of limestone used in York, although more often in the civilian settlements than the fortress, is jurassic oolite which has a distinct bedding plane and as a result is usually found as thin flat slabs. It may have come principally from the North York Moors, although a belt runs through east Yorkshire and reappears in the Lincolnshire Wolds south of the Humber. Finally, the ubiquitous cobbles found in York excavations must also be counted as imports. While small pebbles might originate in the river bed, the cobbles, which can be up to 50 cm (20 in) and more in diameter, would have been created during the last glaciation and were probably quarried on the moraine a few kilometres to the north-west of the fortress.

Transporting the vast quantities of stone to the fortress obviously posed a major logistical problem, but presumably rivers were used rather than roads whenever possible. Millstone

17 *Wooden bowl found underneath the earliest Roman road at Wellington Row (0.20 m scale).*

grit could have been shipped down the river Wharfe from quarries in the Wetherby area. The magnesian limestone could have been brought up the Ouse after a journey over land, or direct from Tadcaster by way of the river Wharfe. The need for a land journey, however short, may explain why the stone rarely occurs in large blocks, but more often in the easily manhandleable smaller ones. Since oolitic limestone mostly occurs in small pieces, it too probably had a land journey before, perhaps, being shipped down the river Derwent from the Roman settlement at Malton.

While one of the principal functions of the legionary *territorium* was the provision of food, it may not always have yielded sufficient and, especially in the early years of the Roman occupation, food was probably imported from southern Britain or even further afield. Bread and cereal would, of course, have been staples and a large quantity of the latter was found in what was probably the remains of a late first-century warehouse on the 39–41 Coney Street site a little to the south of the fortress on the bank of the Ouse (see **32**, 3). On the basis of surviving beam slots it was evident that there had been two phases of timber structure. In deposits associated with the earlier building remains there were some cereal grains, but more remarkable was the large quantity of well-preserved grain beetles. An uncontrollable infestation had probably led to demolition of the building after which the ground was sealed with a thick layer of clay before a new building was erected in its place. In the beam slots of the second phase a large amount of charred grain was found which probably indicates an accidental fire of the sort for which there is also evidence in the civilian settlements (see pp.74–5, 77). Apart from this grain we have little

41

direct evidence for what the soldier at York ate because refuse tips are rarely found in fortress excavations, but at 9 Blake Street the animal bones suggested consumption of smoked or salted shoulders of beef and there is evidence for the preparation of this meat in the *colonia* (see p.82). Trade with the local farmers is difficult to trace, but Dr Jones has suggested that at Naburn it did not begin immediately the Romans arrived as no Roman pottery and glassware from the site can be dated to before the early second century.

While the bulk of their food presumably became, in due course, available locally, the soldiers would have been unwilling to forgo their olive oil and wine. These comestibles arrived in large earthenware jars known as amphorae, numerous pieces of which have been found in York. They show that the oil came largely from southern Spain and the wine from southern Gaul, doubtless including the area of the Rhône valley in which Lucius Duccius Rufinus had grown up.

When local resources failed the legionaries could not only import what they required, as in the case of foodstuffs, but they could also make things themselves. A good example of a commodity manufactured at York by the army is pottery. Although native people in the York area did make pottery, it was not of good quality and the only product was cooking vessels. The legionaries required large quantities of pottery, however, which, because of their alien and sophisticated dining habits, would have consisted of a wide range of vessels including bowls, platters and storage jars as well as flagons for the wine and oil. While each legion's potters had a distinctive style, their products were always in a red earthenware and included several standard forms (**colour plate 5**). Kiln waste has been found on a site on Peaseholme Green (Adam's Hydraulics) which suggests that legionary pottery production in York took place on the south-east side of the fortress where low-lying ground near the Foss was, perhaps, unsuitable for other purposes. The same area has also produced evidence (at the Borthwick Institute site) for the manufacture of roof tiles.

18 *Detail of a cross-section through the second century road surfaces at the Wellington Row site showing the large cobbles at the base and layers of finer gravel above (1m scale).*

A small amount of pottery was imported, in particular the red shiny tableware known as samian which was produced in Gaul. Other vessels of exotic origin, including a number bearing a green glaze, were probably brought by soldiers as personal possessions. Particularly striking was part of a two-handled glazed cup with relief satyrs on it found at the Wellington Row site in the *colonia* (**colour plate 6**). This is a product of kilns in the Lyon area and, although it was recovered from a third-century deposit, the vessel probably dates to the mid-first century. Originally it may have been brought to York by a legionary as a keepsake or souvenir and was then cherished for at least 100 years before being broken and thrown away.

In addition to pottery sherds, fragments of glass vessels have been found in some quantity in the fortress. They were probably all imported, initially from Italy and southern Gaul, but by the late first century from the Rhineland and even from workshops in London. Glass vessels were primarily tableware such as bowls, jars and bottles, but small phials for scented water or other cosmetics are common on military sites including York. One cannot avoid the rather surprising conclusion that, on occasions, Roman soldiers were pleasantly sweet-smelling!

Another group of technical specialists on the legion's staff were the smiths who would have made and serviced weaponry and armour. Unfortunately very little military equipment has been found at York, but a fine bronze helmet cheek-piece, probably of second-century date may be a local product (**19**). In addition, the smiths would have produced large numbers of nails and other structural fittings for the buildings. At 9 Blake Street nails occurred in some quantity in second-century deposits and had presumably been discarded when the timber buildings were replaced in stone. This is one of the most archaeologically visible changes on many sites in the second-century fortress, but the stages in which it occurred and its relationship to other historical events are not easy to understand as we shall see in the next chapter.

19 *Helmet cheek-piece made of copper-alloy, probably second century, found at the Purey Cust site.*

3

The fortress rebuilt

Many readers will be familiar with the historical novels of Rosemary Sutcliff and in particular *The Eagle of the Ninth*. This tells the story of a boy who goes into the wilds of Scotland to search for the truth about the unexplained disappearance of the ninth legion and to recover the sacred eagle standards of the cohort commanded by his father. Until relatively recently, the mystery had some substance to it since there was little evidence for the fate of the legion after 107–8, the date of the great commemorative inscription from King's Square (see **3**), although it was clear that it had departed from York before the arrival of the sixth legion at some time around 120. Since Rosemary Sutcliff published her book in 1954, however, it has become clear that the ninth was still in existence after 120, initially in Lower Germany, where it was based at Nijmegen (today in the Netherlands), and subsequently in the east where it may have been destroyed during a war against the Parthians in 161.

While the departure of the ninth may have been demanded by an emergency in the Rhineland, Britain could not survive for long with only two legions. The arrival of the sixth was, however, specifically occasioned by the visit of the Emperor Hadrian to Britain to secure the northern limit of the province with the wall which bears his name. Much of the legion was probably sent direct to the frontier leaving only a small garrison to move into York.

By the time it arrived in Britain the sixth legion, which bore the title 'victrix', meaning conqueror, had had a long and glorious history going back to Julius Caesar's time in the mid-first century BC when it had served in the Gallic wars. Some hundred years later, in AD 68, the legion was in Spain and subsequently it was transferred under Quintus Petilius Cerialis, commander of the ninth at York in 71, to Germany and the fortress at Neuss. In 89 after supporting the Emperor Domitian against the revolt of Saturninus, the legionary commander in Germany, the legion acquired the title *pia fidelis* (pious and faithful) which appears as PF, along with VIC for *victrix*, on many of the tiles from its York workshop. The exploits of the legion were doubtless handed down from generation to generation of soldiers and kept alive by those at York, a few of whom we know by name from inscriptions.

Roman inscriptions

Before meeting some of the men of the sixth, this is an appropriate point to look at aspects of the form of Roman monumental inscriptions since they make up such an important body of evidence for Roman York. First of all, inscriptions are, for the most part, relatively restricted in their subject matter being principally commemorations of public works, or funerary and religious dedications. They are also fairly standardized in terms of the type of information they convey. If, for example, the inscription is from a privately-sponsored building or monument there is usually great emphasis on the status of the individual responsible, while in officially-inspired inscriptions the emperor and his titles feature prominently. The lack of variety in subject matter and content allowed the employment of stock words or phrases, and since everyone who mattered would know what these were, inscriptions could, if only to save space, be radically abbreviated so that most are in a sort of code. Examples of such abbreviations on York inscriptions include the obvious

LEG for legion and AUG for Augustus (emperor), but in addition we find DM on many sarcophagi standing for *Dis Manibus*, 'to the spirits of the dead', and on altars the last line is often VSLM meaning *Votum Solvit Libens Merito* which is translated as 'willingly and deservedly paid his vow'.

Abbreviation was also applied to names, but the complete form is usually readily apparent. A male citizen would have the right to possess the *tria nomina* (three names) which consisted of a *praenomen*, or personal name, the *nomen gentilicium* or *nomen*, a family name, and a *cognomen* or private name. A good example of the *tria nomina* from York are those of the standard-bearer Lucius Duccius Rufinus. As there were relatively few *praenomina* they were usually abbreviated to one or two letters: L for Lucius, Ti for Tiberius for example. This lack of variety also meant that as time went on the *praenomen* was gradually dropped as it was not very useful for distinguishing between individuals. On York inscriptions it is most common to find just two names, the *nomen* and the *cognomen*.

Female citizens usually had two names – Julia Brica on a tombstone from York is typical (see **56**) – the family name followed by the private one. Both names often bore a close resemblance to those of the woman's father. The daughter of Julia Brica was, for example, named Sempronia Martina after her father Sempronius Martinus. This tombstone also shows, however, that a Roman woman's name did not necessarily change when she married. Non-citizens and slaves are rarely mentioned in inscriptions, but usually had one name, sometimes accompanied by that of their father.

While Roman names can tell us a certain amount about a person's social status, they may also convey other information, including the time when the family received citizenship. On becoming a citizen a man would usually take the *nomen* of the reigning emperor. In Britain Flavius (and Flavia), and Aelius (and Aelia) are common, being the *nomina* of, respectively, the Flavian emperors – Vespasian, Titus and Domitian – and of Hadrian. Particularly common, however, is Aurelius (and Aurelia), the *nomen* of Caracalla (211–17) who granted citizenship to all free-born inhabitants of the empire. To some extent this was a recognition that citizenship had become so widespread that it no longer counted as a

meaningful privilege but it also allowed the state to levy more taxes as citizens paid more than non-citizens. Finally, a Roman name can also indicate an individual's regional origins even if it has been latinized. The *cognomina* of Julia Brica and Candida Barita from York are, for example, thought to be native British.

Of the men who commanded the sixth legion, only three are known by name, although the post-holder probably changed every three years. Two of these commanders are known from York itself and one on Hadrian's Wall. Of the two from York one was named Quintus Antonius Isauricus and he is referred to on an altar dedicated to the goddess Fortuna by his wife Sosia Juncina found on the site of the baths in north-west part of the *colonia*. This inscription is of interest not only because of the legate's name and the dedication – entirely appropriate to a soldier's wife – but because it is a relatively rare example of an altar set up by a woman. In a society where men dominated public life there were few women, other than those of Sosia Juncina's elevated status, who were able to breach the male preserve of sponsoring stone monuments.

The second legate known from York is Claudius Hieronymianus whose name appears on the commemorative inscription he placed in a temple of Serapis (see **2**), also located in the *colonia*. Another senior man from the sixth legion was Antonius Gargillianus whose tombstone was found at the Minster where it had been reused for an Anglo-Saxon grave. This man had been the camp prefect at York and was of equestrian rank. From the less elevated levels of legionary society we know of a number of centurions including Aurelius Super whose sarcophagus was commissioned by his widow Aurelia Censorina (**20**); their names suggest membership of a family which had acquired citizenship under Caracalla. We may also note that Aurelius Super is recorded as dying at the age of 38 and he is one of the many people referred to on York's funerary inscriptions who died in their mid to late thirties. Of particular interest for the light that it casts on the communications between the sixth legion and the rest of the Roman world is an altar set up by Marcus Minucius Mudenus (**21**) who refers to himself as a *gubernator* or river pilot, and he presumably assisted ships bringing supplies and troops up the Ouse. The diverse sources of such cargoes are hinted at by the dedication to the Mother

20 *Coffin of the centurion Aurelius Super who lived for 38 years, 4 months and 13 days –* QVI VIXIT AN(N) IS XXXVIII M(ENSES) IIII D(IES) XIII). *The coffin/memorial was put in place by his wife Aurelia Censorina –* AVRELIA CENSORINA CONIVNX MEMORIAM POSSVIT. *Found in Castle Yard in 1835.*

Goddesses of Africa, Italy and Gaul. Finally, we may note the tombstone of a serving legionary named Lucius Baebius Crescens who is a good example of a recruit from a province created, like Britain, late in the Roman era of expansion. He came from *Augusta Vindelicorum* (Augsburg), a *colonia* and the capital of Raetia close to the German frontier.

Rebuilding and replanning
The second century witnessed many changes both in the overall organization of the fortress at York and in the form of individual buildings, but determining the exact historical context in which these changes took place is not an easy matter. To some extent this is because of the inadequate records of early excavations, but a much more serious obstacle to exact dating lies in the nature of the archaeological evidence itself.

In the superimposed layers of building debris, refuse and so forth which make up York's archaeology there are large quantities of discarded artefacts. As far as Roman sites are concerned, by far the most numerous are pieces of broken pottery, but in addition there are objects of metal, bone, glass and other materials. The types of artefact in use, and their form and composition, changed over time. By studying ancient artefacts in relation to the sequences of layers in which they were found it is possible to establish the relative sequence in which these changes occurred and create what are usually known as typologies. Some artefacts, notably certain types of pottery, are particularly susceptible to change and in the

21 (*Above*) *Altar to the mother goddesses of Africa, Italy and Gaul dedicated by Marcus Minucius Mudenus, a gubernator (river pilot) of the sixth legion. Found in Micklegate in 1752.*

22 (*Right*) *Composite plan of the fortress at York showing the completed circuit of stone defences and principal stone buildings. (Recorded structures shown darkest, conjectured structures shown lighter, structures recorded on 1852 O.S. map, but possibly incorrect shown hatched).*

ROMAN YORK

22 (p. 49) Due to a printing error the Roman plan was wrongly superimposed on the modern streets. The correct version is given here.

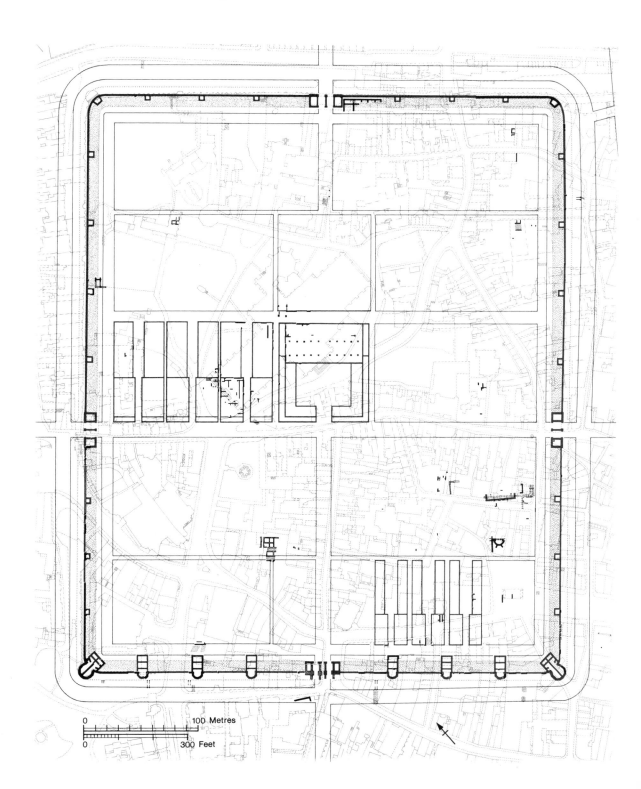

0 ————— 100 Metres
0 ————— 300 Feet

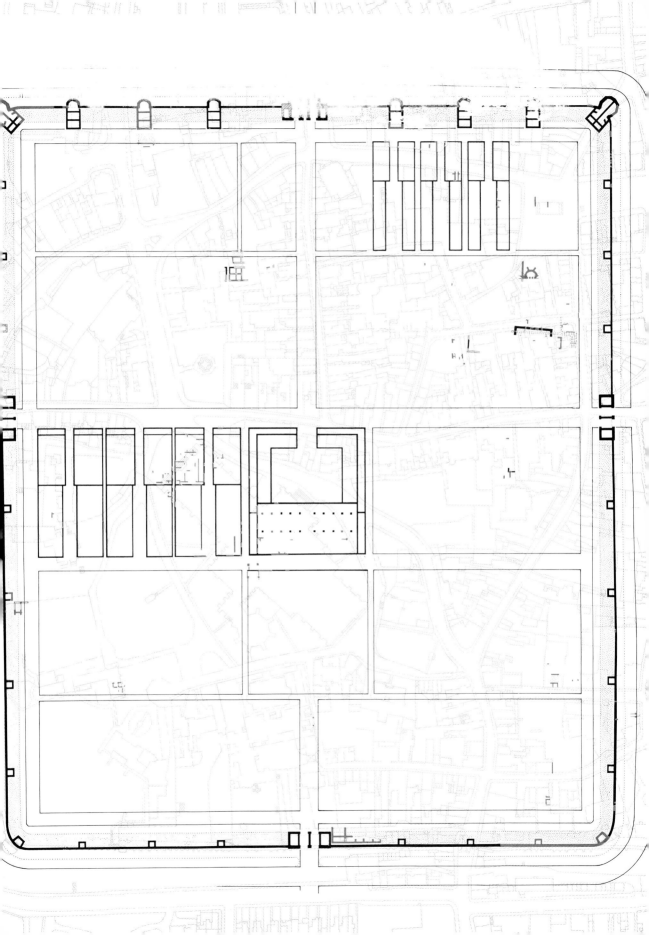

earlier part of the Roman period this is especially true of samian ware. As a result of intensive research, the manufacture of many individual pieces can be dated to within 10–20 years.

While sequences of superimposed layers may provide the raw material for typologies of pottery and other artefacts, it is more difficult to give real dates to the stages of development they illustrate and thus to date the events for which evidence is found in excavations. One route to solving the problem of dating archaeological discoveries in the Roman period is the use of coins since, although they do not actually have calendar dates stamped on them, they usually bear sufficient information to allow dating of their production to within a few years, if not a single year. In certain periods during the Roman era, especially parts of the late third and fourth centuries, very large numbers of coins were minted and they are common site finds.

The whole question of dating is, however, complicated by the fact that a particular coin or pottery sherd may have been redeposited many times before reaching its final resting place, especially in somewhere like York which has been intensively occupied over many centuries. During this time the ground has been continuously dug over for pits and ditches, or scraped up for use in structures like the reconstructed fortress rampart (see p.59). In any group of finds from an archaeological layer there will, therefore, be many of an earlier, often a considerably earlier, date than the creation of the layer itself. The archaeologist's job is to spot the latest artefact and then try to work out when it was produced. Even if numerous coins and samian fragments are found, however, the redeposition factor reduces the possibility of giving an exact date to any layer or structure. As far as Roman York is concerned, we are usually lucky to be confident to within a range of 20 to 30 years. It is more common to talk in 50 year ranges, or to be relatively sure about one end of a date range, usually the earlier. Because it changed relatively slowly, the degree of uncertainty is greatest if locally-made pottery, rather than coins or samian, is the only material available for dating. As the supply of samian ended in the early third century, later Roman deposits and structures in York may be particularly difficult to date given the present state of knowledge.

Considerable attention in recent years has been directed to scientific techniques which appear to offer some solution to this problem of dating and do not rely on the judgement of the archaeologist. Radiocarbon dating has received the greatest attention, but for Roman sites it cannot provide the degree of precision required, and the most useful technique is probably dendrochronology. This involves matching the pattern of growth rings on an ancient timber to a master pattern or 'curve' which has been dated by radiocarbon or other means. The survival of suitable timbers is by no means common; it relies on the sort of waterlogged ground conditions which only occur in certain parts of York. Although dendrochronology has been extensively employed on Anglo-Scandinavian timbers from the city, it has as yet not been of great value for the Roman period. Structural timbers have been found in the *colonia*, if not in the fortress, but there is insufficient comparative material to create a datable 'curve' for York.

Any statement in this book about the dating of the developments in both the Roman fortress and civilian settlements at York constitutes the best estimate that can be given at present. Further work on pottery, coins and dendrochronology is sure to allow greater refinement in the future. There will, however, always be a measure of uncertainty about the date of even the major events for which we have archaeological evidence and relating them to written history will usually involve an element of speculation.

New work on the defences
The examination of changes to the fortress may begin with the defences in the east quadrant. Excavations at Aldwark in 1971–2 by Peter Wenham revealed more of Interval Tower NE6, first exposed by Miller in the 1920s. Wenham showed that the tower had probably been built in the reign of Trajan (98–117) or Hadrian (117–38). It appeared to pre-date the fortress curtain wall, which still survives in this area.

The east corner tower (23) may be contemporary with NE6 as it too appears to pre-date the

23 *The east corner of the fortress showing the wall built in the late second or early third century and remains of the earlier tower. The medieval city wall is at the top.*

standing fortress wall. It is possible that work began on a curtain wall at this period, although it was not accompanied by work on the rampart, the reconstruction of which is clearly later. A short stretch of wall standing a few courses high found by Miller at his Hawarden Place site was thought by the Royal Commission to be Trajanic. It had no distinctive plinth comparable to the later second/early third-century wall at the east corner (see p.58) and the foundations were of clay and cobble over short timber piles with a form of concrete buttress (see **27**).

Directly comparable foundations, but no surviving upstanding wall, were found in Bedern Trench 3/4 and at 7–9 Aldwark. At the east corner the wall foundation trench had been dug deeper and wider than elsewhere as one would expect at a point of stress, and the clay and cobble was capped with concrete. Northwest of the corner the wall foundations were concrete or mortared rubble. If one accepts the distinction in foundation type as indicating work of different periods, then it may be suggested that an early second-century curtain wall ran from the east corner for a restricted distance along the south-east side of the fortress. At present, however, in the absence of any dating evidence for the Hawarden Place wall and associated foundations, it is equally likely that the addition of a wall to the defences in the east quadrant of the fortress was contemporary throughout with the reconstruction of the rampart which took place in the late second or early third century (see pp.58–9), although this would imply that tower NE6 and the east corner tower were initially built freestanding.

Another piece of evidence which has been advanced as proof of a Trajanic fortress wall was the King's Square inscription (see **3**) which, it has been suggested, came from the *porta principalis sinistra*. This is clearly possible given its find spot, but even if it did commemorate a new gateway, there is no compelling reason why it should have been accompanied by a curtain wall.

Buildings in the *intervallum*

The second important change to the fortress which was probably initiated, if not completed, in the first quarter of the second century was the construction of buildings in the *intervallum* between the rampart and the *via sagularis*,

which by analogy with other British fortresses were probably intended as stores and cook houses. Apart from the baths and the *principia*, these are the first buildings in stone in the fortress at York and traces have been found at the following sites (the likely date of construction given in brackets): Aldwark 1971–2 (early second century), Davygate (early second century), Judge's Lodgings (second century), Interval Tower SW5 (mid-second century), Interval Tower NW5 (?second century), Dean's Park (unknown).

The construction of *intervallum* buildings may have been intimately related to another major change in fortress plan, the widening of the space for the rampart and *intervallum* which took place at some stage in the second century. In the late first-century fortress this space was 16.3 m (53 ft) wide, of which *c.* 6 m (20 ft) was occupied by the rampart. By the later second century it was *c.* 22 m (72 ft) in the *praetentura*, and where recorded on the north-east and south-east sides of the *retentura* the new distance was as much as 25 m (82 ft). In the east quadrant the reconstructed rampart was *c.* 10 m (33 ft) wide (see pp.58–9).

Dating this reorganization poses a problem which the available evidence is simply not good enough to solve at present. As already noted, it may accompany the construction of *intervallum* buildings early in the second century or, alternatively, it may accompany the reconstruction and widening of the rampart, and general reconstruction of the fortress buildings in stone, which mostly appears to begin in the mid-second century. Another possibility is that the widening could have been a two-stage process, with the building line moved inwards before the construction of the new rampart, which in some cases covered abandoned *intervallum* buildings.

At all events, the widening of the *intervallum* clearly involved the removal of buildings on the periphery of the fortress and there is some evidence for this taking place at the Aldwark/Bedern sites in the first quarter of the second century. Demolition was carefully executed; the timbers were probably withdrawn for reuse and the beam slots were backfilled with clay. In the deposits immediately overlying the slots there was burnt material, possibly a result of the disposal of unreusable refuse. One interpretation of the pottery evidence is that the ground was left open for 20–30 years before reconstruction in stone took place in the 150s or 160s.

Whatever the exact date of the widening of the *intervallum* and demolition of the Aldwark/Bedern buildings, the evidence, principally in the form of relative quantities of pottery, from all the sites studied in the fortress suggests that there was a decrease in the level of activity between *c.* 120 and *c.* 150. This must be related to the posting of most of the sixth legion to Hadrian's Wall and subsequently the Antonine Wall frontier in Scotland. Around the middle of the second century, however, it is clear that a major programme of reconstructing the buildings and defences in stone was set in train.

Methods of construction

The types and sources of stone used in Roman York have already been discussed, and before looking any further at the new buildings it is useful to look at how the Romans went about using the material. While drystone walling is known from pre-Roman times in Britain, the mortared stone wall was an innovation of the Romans and allowed the construction of buildings of far greater architectural ambition than anything hitherto seen.

The stability of Roman stone buildings depended, of course, on the quality of the foundations. In York they were usually set in trenches up to about 0.50–1 m deep (1 ft 8 in–3 ft 4 in), sufficient to protect them from the destructive effects of freezing and thawing in the winter. Clay with cobbles was a favoured foundation material, especially in military buildings, but in civilian contexts there are also examples of the use of limestone slabs, set on edge to ensure the easy drainage of ground water. Two other foundation materials which have only been recorded in the fortress wall are, firstly, concrete and, secondly, limestone fragments in a mortar matrix.

Mortar and concrete were made in much the same way, the crucial ingredient being lime. This was produced by a process known as calcination which involves heating limestone to *c.* 1000°C (1832°F) in a special kiln. The resulting lime is a powdery material, but water was added to form a paste known as slaked lime which could be used for building. Both mortar and concrete used a mixture of lime, sand and aggregate, usually cobbles and pebbles, but in different proportions. Mortar has more sand, but less aggregate and lime

compared to concrete. Since lime was rather more expensive than the other components, there was a tendency to economize on it with the result that many Roman buildings, especially in the civilian settlements, had poorly bonded walls. The concrete and mortar in the fortress wall footings was, however, very hard indeed and has defeated modern demolition equipment on several occasions. A clay and cobble mix could be laid directly into the foundation trenches, but since fresh mortar or concrete was in semi-liquid form it was poured into a timber framework, known as shuttering, within the trench to enable it to set in a tidy, solid block with a smooth and level surface.

Another component of Roman building foundations, frequently found in York, is timber piles which were driven into the base of the trench to ensure the stability of the wall above. The Romans found that the subsoil under much of York was unstable being sand or silty clay, with matters possibly being made worse by a high water-table, even though we know it was appreciably lower in Roman times than it is today. The timber piles, usually oak, can reach up to 3 m (10 ft) in length and 50 cm (20 in) in thickness, but it is more common to find them 0.50–1 m (20 in–3 ft 4 in) in length and 10–20 cm (4–8 in) thick.

Some Roman walls in York had their lower courses made of large gritstone blocks, but the principal construction technique for stone walls, as elsewhere in Rome's north-western provinces, employed narrow facing courses, of limestone in York's case, with a mortared rubble core. This is often known as *opus vittatum*, a term which derives from the word *vitta*, a head band. The usual method of wall building was probably to proceed upwards in stages of a given height, starting each with the core and then adding the facing; most blocks were tapered to allow them to be pushed easily into place (see **25**). To construct walls of a height greater than a person's reach, scaffolding was required and this usually involved a timber framework which would be secured by the wall itself (**colour plate 10**). By leaving out some of the facing stones cross-members could be inserted into the wall or, alternatively, poles were passed through the complete thickness of the wall to hold a scaffold frame on either side. The holes in the wall face, known as putlog holes, were sometimes filled in as scaffolding was taken down, but were often left open and appear to have been considered a decorative feature. Good examples of putlog holes in York can still be seen on the inner face of the Multangular Tower.

The Romans' use of masonry and lime mortar was accompanied by the development of protective plaster wall coverings. At their simplest they usually consisted of three coats, the first was relatively thick, typically 3–5 cm (1–2 in), consisting of lime and coarse sand with a roughened surface to take the second layer, a mortar using fine sand, which was smoothed off to take the final layer of lime wash, on which any decorative scheme was painted. To ensure against the paint fading, the basic colour scheme was usually applied when the plaster was still wet, a technique known as fresco. The evidence from York is that decoration was largely simple, the commonest pattern being one or two coloured stripes on a white background. On occasions, however, more elaborate designs were executed on dry plaster using a painting technique known as tempera. The paint was given adhesive qualities by mixing it with a glue made of egg white.

A common form of decoration, used at York and elsewhere, was imitation three-dimensional panelling (**colour plate 7**). This would consist of a dado for the first metre or so above the floor, often painted in imitation of marble. Above this was a central section showing recessed panels, with a cornice moulding depicted above, and finally a frieze. Both the recessed panels and the frieze might be painted with a range of naturalistic motifs, such as flowers and animals, or mythological scenes. On fragments of plaster from a house on the 37 Bishophill site in the *colonia* there were parts of human figures and stylized plants, but the most elaborate decoration on wall plaster from York has come from the fortress headquarters in a room added on the north-west side of the basilica in the early fourth century. Above an elaborate marbled dado there is a series of panels interrupted by niches defined by classical columns. The frieze is also panelled and at one point a tragic mask is depicted.

Moving from the walls to the floors, the best known Roman form is, of course, the mosaic pavement and there are a few examples from the civilian settlements at York (see pp.102–6). In the majority of cases, however, floors appear to have been more simple. Although the basilica

of the fortress headquarters had a stone-flagged floor, military buildings usually had floors of beaten earth, clay, or *opus signinum*, a form of concrete incorporating tile fragments to give it waterproof qualities (see **25**). In the civilian town there are also examples of mortar and timber floors (see pp.74–5).

The roofs of York's Roman buildings are the part about which least is known since none, of course, survives. Some kind of timber framework would usually have been employed, however, and by analogy with evidence for roofs at Pompeii and elsewhere we may imagine that at York they were based on triangular trusses which in turn supported horizontal purlins. Rafters would be fixed to the purlins and would bear a waterproof cladding. In the fortress this usually took the form of clay tiles arranged as lines of rectangular *tegulae* which ran down the roof slope, the upper overlapping the lower, with the junctions between the lines covered by semi-circular *imbrices*. York excavations also produce large numbers of thin sandstone

24 *Moulded terracotta antefix from a gable end.*

slabs which in many cases can be identified as roofing material as they are pierced at one side to allow attachment to the rafters by an iron pin. These slabs are of stone known to geologists as Elland Flag, but often described today as York Stone. The source is in the Leeds/Bradford/Huddersfield area of West Yorkshire. Roof pitch would, as in Mediterranean countries today, have been quite low, probably about 20 degrees from the horizontal.

With this summary of construction techniques in mind, we may turn to the remains of fortress buildings on the ground. The headquarters building was, as we have already noted, built in stone at the beginning of the second century and there is no evidence for major changes in plan until the fourth century. The bath house, however, has been shown by recent excavations at Back Swinegate to have been reconstructed in the mid-second century, but few details were apparent as the trenches were very restricted in area.

Barracks

As far as barracks are concerned, the Davygate site in the *praetentura* produced fragments of stone structures which were thought to be second century, but could not be dated more closely. It is likely, however, that the *intervallum* widening had meant a reduction in the length of the barracks by about 16 per cent to *c.* 66 m (216 ft) from the *c.* 78 m (256 ft) they had been in the late first century. The width of a pair of stone barracks at Davygate (including the alley separating it from the next pair) was *c.* 31.5 m (103 ft/105 pM) as opposed to a suggested *c.* 25 m (82 ft/85 pM) for the earlier timber barracks (see pp.34–7). The new width appears to be confirmed by the discoveries at 9 Blake Street (see below). Since the maximum amount of space available for the stone barracks between the *via praetoria* and the realigned *intervallum* was probably *c.* 173 m (568 ft/585 pM), it is clear that the usual six pairs could not be fitted in if they were all of the same size. How the problem was resolved is unknown, but it must remain a possibility that there were fewer barracks in the replanned fortress than there had been previously. Little is known of the stone barracks and other buildings in the Aldwark/Bedern area as only a few fragments were revealed in the excavations.

In discussing the late first-century timber structures at 9 Blake Street we have already seen that there were two ranges, one of which was identified as living quarters and the other as a service wing with a kitchen, and this arrangement appears to be repeated after reconstruction in stone (**25–26a**). The plan of the stone structures is, moreover, much better preserved than that of their timber predecessors and by identifying the likely measurements in Roman feet it is possible to suggest the principles on which they were laid out.

The corners of two stone barrack blocks were located at the south-west corner of the site, and allowing for a portico 10 pM wide along the *via praetoria* it would have been possible to fit a pair 105 pM wide, or slightly more, into the space north-west of the portico. North-east of the barracks ran the north-west/south-east street which was 10 pM wide, with the two ranges of buildings next to it. Working from south-west to north-east we find that the overall width was probably 52.5 pM ($1\frac{1}{2} \times 35$), the service range being 15 pM wide, the alley 7.5 pM wide and the main block 30 pM wide. A pleasing hierarchy of dimensions is therefore apparent: the residential range was twice the width of the service range which was twice the width of the alley which was in turn $\frac{3}{4}$ the width of the street on the south-west.

Working across the site from the north-west to the south-east there is the wall of a building which mostly lies beyond the site; this is followed by an alley 5 pM wide and then the north-west wall of the building of which we know most. It is 30 pM to the next major building line after which is a possible cobbled yard or passage. The distance from the north-west edge of the alley to the north-west edge of the presumed portico along the *via praetoria* is 150 pM and it can be conjectured that this was divided into two 75 pM units, each designed to be occupied by a building 70 pM (2×35) long and alley 5 pM wide, perhaps as shown in **26b**. It may also be noted that the diagonal across a building unit 70 pM $\times$ 52.5 pM is 87.5 pM ($2\frac{1}{2} \times 35$). Some additional evidence for this conjectured layout was found in a small trench excavated to the south-east of the main site where it appears that there was a wall running north-west/south-east on the line of the south-west wall of the residential range.

At some stage, which cannot be closely dated, the principal room at 9 Blake Street was divided into four smaller rooms, but whether this meant a change in building function is unclear. Before

25 *Stone buildings at 9 Blake Street looking north-west. In the foreground is the main room in the residential block with the* opus signinum *floors and secondary dividing walls clearly visible.*

leaving 9 Blake Street two unusual discoveries should be noted. The first consisted of 35 silver coins in a restricted area of the footings of the south-east wall of the principal room. They dated from between 66 BC and AD 79, the latter date being some 70 years or so earlier than the

pottery date for the building. It is possible either that the coins were treasured possessions which had been kept for this period of time before being buried intentionally as an offering for the good fortune of the building or, more likely, that they had been disturbed from an earlier hoard and then, perhaps, reburied for fear of offending the gods. The second unusual discovery was a human infant skeleton buried early in the life of the building in the floor of the principal room. The burial of infants in Roman buildings is a well-known phenomenon, although rare in a military context, and, in this

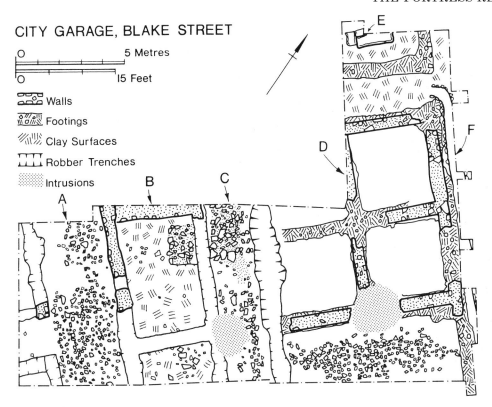

CITY GARAGE, BLAKE STREET

O ——————— 5 Metres

O ——————— I5 Feet

Walls

Footings

Clay Surfaces

Robber Trenches

Intrusions

A

B

C

D

E

F

a

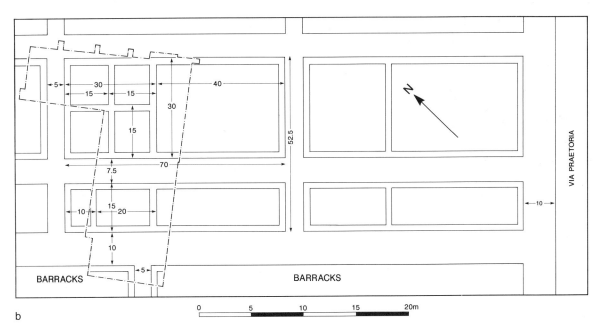

5
30
15
15
40
30
15
52.5
7.5
70
10
15
20
10
5

BARRACKS

BARRACKS

N

VIA PRAETORIA

10

0   5   10   15   20m

b

26 *9 Blake Street – a) Plan showing the stone buildings as found. Key: A = street, B = service wing, C = passage, D = residential block, E = cistern, F = drain.*

b) A theoretical reconstruction of the intended layout including the adjacent area to the south-east – measurements in Roman feet.

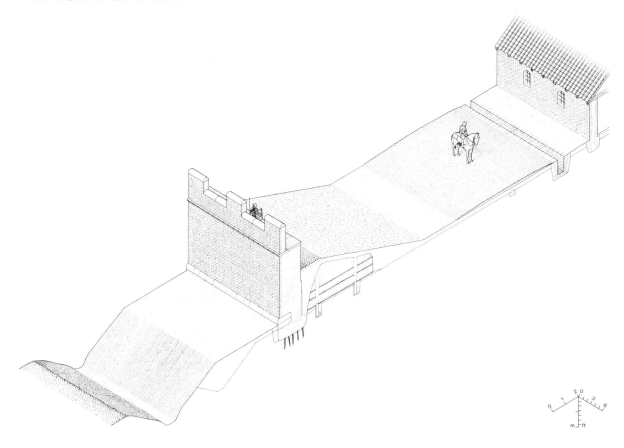

27 *A hypothetical reconstruction of the late second-/early third-century fortress defences south-west of the east corner.*

case, can again be interpreted as a form of votive offering to encourage the gods to look favourably on the residents. We presume that the infant died of natural causes and was not a deliberate sacrifice.

The reconstructed defences

While some work on the defences had taken place in the early second century, much more extensive reconstruction began in the last quarter of the second or first quarter of the third. This involved redigging the fortress ditch on a new line, building a stone curtain wall and widening the rampart. The new arrangement as it may have been completed in the east quadrant of the fortress south-west of the east corner is shown in **27**.

The evidence for the re-cut ditch comes, as

in the case of the first ditch, only from sections at Interval Towers SW5 and SW6 where it appears that a new line was established *c.* 5.3 m (17 ft 6 in), measured centre to centre, outside the first ditch. The new ditch was *c.* 6 m (19 ft 6 in) wide and 2.80 m (9 ft) deep, and between its inner edge and the wall the berm was probably *c.* 5.9 m (18 ft) wide.

In the east quadrant of the fortress the wall itself (the foundations are described on p.52) was usually *c.* 1.5 m (5 ft) thick at the base, but as much as 2.2 m (7 ft) thick at the east corner. The plinth at the east corner was made of large blocks of millstone grit surmounted by a course of chamfered limestone blocks which can still be seen today, as can the courses of small limestone blocks making up the main body of the wall (see **23**). These blocks are finely jointed on the exterior and more crudely jointed and less even on the interior where, of course, they would have been hidden behind the rampart. At the east corner the wall still stands *c.* 5 m (16 ft 6 in) high and at the top there is a projecting cornice. Rising above this there

28 *Cross-section through the realigned fortress ditch of the late second/early third-century at Interval Tower SW5 looking south-east (the scale is 0.50 m). The base of the first ditch is the slight step to the right of centre. The deeper ditch is the first recut, note the typical military profile with an 'ankle-breaking' slot at the base to aid cleaning-out.*

would originally have been the wall of the corner tower.

It seems clear from the Aldwark excavations in 1971–2 that the rampart was reconstructed at the same time as the wall was built. The upper 1 m ($3\frac{1}{4}$ ft) or so of the old rampart had been removed; the new one was made up to much same height of *c.* 3 m (10 ft), but was widened from the original 6 m (19 ft 6 in) to *c.* 10 m (33 ft). The make-up of the new rampart was rather mixed material, probably deriving in part from redigging the fortress ditch and in part from redeposition of the earlier rampart. It is in dating this second rampart and by association the wall itself that serious problems arise since it will be clear from the redeposited nature of the rampart make-up that much of the pottery in it could have been discarded many years earlier. There is, however, enough pottery from both the rampart and the back-filled wall construction trench at Aldwark 1971–2 to indicate a later second- or early third-century date for the redesigned defences in the east quadrant of the fortress.

Outside the east quadrant there is no evidence for a wall comparable to that just described except for a short stretch found in a sewer trench in Parliament Street in 1976 and in the basement of an adjacent property, 16 Parliament Street, in 1987. The latter discovery

29 *YAT Excavation Assistant Mike Burley examining the late second-/early third century fortress wall at 16 Parliament Street. The basement floor level is at the top right.*

30 *Detail of the fortress wall plinth at 16 Parliament Street showing stone tooling marks.*

took place in one of the Archaeological Trust's more unusual excavations which arose because of the need for underpinning work in the standing building. This had become unstable because one half rested on the solid fortress wall and the other on the soft infilling of the fortress ditch. When the basement floor was taken up, the fortress wall appeared directly underneath it (**29**). Excavation in advance of the insertion of new ground beams showed that the wall was still standing 2 m (6 ft 6 in) high, in immaculate condition.

The wall in the sewer trench and at 16 Parliament Street had a distinctive plinth of a type not previously recorded at York (**30**). It had a projecting base course of large limestone blocks and then a chamfered course, above which the stones were decorated with unusual vertical grooves and criss-cross patterns. This plinth is similar but not identical in form to the plinth at the east corner, but it is more like the plinth of the fortress wall at Chester, recently re-dated to *c.* 200, and the plinth of the southern extension of the fort at South Shields which is associated with the campaigns of the Emperor Septimius Severus in 211. The extent of the wall with the Parliament Street plinth is not known, but it did not go beyond the south corner of the fortress or, it seems, as far as the *porta principalis sinistra* since a site to the south-west of the gate at King's Square produced a stretch of wall in the style associated with the later third century (see pp.97–100).

In conclusion, a re-examination of the archaeology of the fortress defences, taking into account evidence from recent excavations, appears to demand a revision of the sequence of reconstruction proposed by the Royal Commission. While some stone towers and possibly a stone south-east gate were built in the Trajanic-Hadrianic period, it is unlikely that there was a contemporary curtain wall except, perhaps, in a restricted area south-west of the east corner. In the late second or early third century work began or was continued, but was not completed, on a wall accompanied by a new ditch and a redesigned rampart.

The next episode of work on the defences, which involved erecting a wall and towers around the circuit outside the east quadrant (except in the Parliament Street area), has been traditionally dated to the late third or early fourth century. Since there is, it seems, no good evidence that this work replaced an earlier wall, we would now have to accept that, if that dating is correct, the reconstruction of the fortress defences was abandoned for at least 50 or even as much as 100 years.

The implied picture of a third-century fortress with a part-completed wall co-existing with largely unmodified late first-century structures is, to say the least, surprising in view of what we assume to be the role of York as one of Britain's great Roman bases. None the less, the idea of a gap in the work on the defences does allow York to be compared with military sites elsewhere in northern Britain in the mid-third century, which appear to exhibit a low level of activity if not actual dereliction. A possible context for the cessation of work on the York defences might be the death of the Emperor Septimius Severus in 211 which was followed by a rapid end to his British campaign, but, as already noted, it is rarely possible to relate archaeological evidence to historically documented events with any degree of confidence. In considering this problem of the fortress wall we should also note the expense involved in constructing major stone structures. This is probably a crucial factor which separated the initiation and completion of town walls in both the Roman and medieval periods by a gap of 100 years and possibly even more on some occasions.

Septimius Severus in York
Although it is difficult to relate any specific archaeological discoveries in York to the visit of Septimius Severus in 209–11, the events of

these years are of interest in their own right, especially as they have been a lasting source of civic pride in more recent times. The same William Hargrove who was quoted in Chapter 1 asserted, for example, that 'it was during this residence of Severus that our city shone in its full splendour', while in 1956 Peter Wenham commented on the emperor's funeral in the *Short Guide to Roman York* with the words: 'In some sense that vivid spectacle marked a turning point in the history of the civilized world and York was its setting.'

Severus' intention in coming to York was to use the fortress as a base for punitive campaigns against the Caledonian tribes in the north of Britain who, it has been suggested, had attacked some of the forts both north of Hadrian's Wall and on the Wall itself in the early years of the third century. If such was the case, the Romans would, of course, have regarded retribution as warranted and may even have had some notion of returning the British frontier to the line of the Antonine Wall. It is still a little surprising that Severus did not leave the campaign to his governor, but came to Britain in person at a time when he was over 60 and in poor health. Having spent most of his life on campaign, however, Severus may have grown accustomed to the thrill of military triumphs and felt the need to show there was life in the old man yet. It would also seem in keeping with the character of the emperor that he may simply have been curious to see the remote British province which was about as far from his North African birthplace at Lepcis Magna as it was possible to go without crossing the empire's frontiers. In addition, the contemporary writer Cassius Dio implies that Severus wanted to get his sons away from an idle life in Rome. The emperor probably felt that experience of the rigours of a campaign and the gloss of a military triumph would improve the young men's prospects of ensuring succession to the throne after their father's death.

Severus would have travelled to York with a huge retinue as the empire's seat of government was wherever the emperor happened to be. As proof of this we know of decrees issued at York for quite mundane matters, such as, for example, the right of a lady in Rome named Caecilia to recover possession of some slaves or servants. During their stay in York the imperial family are reported in one source to have resided in a palace or *domus palatina*. No trace of such a building has ever been found, but while it may be revealed one day, it is, perhaps, more likely that the legionary legate's house was used. Reference to the imperial family prompts us to recall that Severus was accompanied to Britain by his empress Julia Domna, a priest's daughter from Emesa in Syria, and by their sons Geta and Caracalla; the latter accompanied his father in the north. Caracalla had been declared co-emperor in 198 and Geta was promoted in 209. This led to considerable rivalry between the brothers which must have intensified as Severus' health deteriorated.

Matters came to head on 2 February 211 when the emperor died in York. His death was not altogether unexpected, it seems, as quite apart from his illness, Severus had been warned by numerous dreams and omens. According to one account, the most vivid warning came after a visit to a temple of Bellona when, in error, some black, rather than the customary white animals had been prepared for sacrifice. On leaving the temple in dismay Severus then found the animals followed him home thus confirming his worst fears. The emperor's death was evidently followed by a splendid cremation and funeral after which his ashes were shipped back to Rome. Julia Domna, Caracalla and Geta left Britain with precipitate haste to secure the crown with all thoughts of further conquest in Scotland forgotten.

4

The civilian settlements

From the time of its foundation the Roman fortress at York would have exercised a powerful influence on the lives of the local people. On the one hand the soldiers would have regarded them as a source of manual labour, food and other supplies. On the other hand many members of the native community probably saw the requirements of the army as an opportunity for personal enrichment. It is in this relationship of mutual dependence that we may find the origin of the permanent civilian settlements at York. As time went on the relationship remained close, but it continued to evolve as historical circumstances changed.

In the late first and early second centuries the land adjacent to the fortress on both sides of the Ouse would have been under strict military supervision, but in due course this was relaxed and the civilians acquired a substantial amount of autonomy to run their own affairs. By the end of the fourth century there may have been little distinction between the status of people living inside and outside the fortress as the army disintegrated in the twilight years of the western empire.

Autonomy may be considered as a fundamental characteristic of a town, but, before we can describe the Roman civilian settlements at York as a town, the concept itself requires some further discussion. Although most people in Britain today live in towns and might feel they know what a town is, it is none the less difficult to give a clear-cut definition of what sets a town apart from other settlements. Factors such as population size, economic and social role, amenities and internal organization must all be taken into consideration and may be given different emphasis according to historical circumstances. As far as the Roman period is concerned towns are usually defined, first of all, as places with a distinct legal status which acted as centres of government and administration for their regions. These places were not, however, a homogeneous group, but were incorporated into the Roman social and governmental system by being graded according to the rights and privileges of their inhabitants. This grading was reflected in the nature and variety of the amenities the place possessed. At the lowest level were the capitals of the *civitates*, the self-governing regions within a province whose boundaries were based on those of the pre-Roman population. The vast majority of the inhabitants of the *civitates* were noncitizens known as *peregrini* (aliens). The next grade up was the *municipium* in which the inhabitants might have so-called 'latin rights' giving them higher status than the *peregrini*. Verulamium (St Albans) is the only certain example of a *municipium* in Britain, although the fourth-century writer Aurelius Victor described York as a *municipium* at the time of Septimius Severus' visit.

The highest level in the urban hierarchy was the *colonia* (colony). Some part, at least, of the civilian settlement at York had acquired this title by 237, the date of an altar dedicated at Bordeaux by Marcus Aurelius Lunaris who described himself as a *sevir augustalis*, or priest of the cult of the emperor, at the *coloniae* of both York and Lincoln (**31**). A possible historical context for York's promotion to *colonia* status

31 *The millstone grit altar dedicated at Bordeaux in 237 to the Tutela Boudiga by Marcus Aurelius Lunaris,* sevir augustalis *of the* coloniae *at York and Lincoln.*

is its establishment as the capital of the province of *Britannia Inferior* (Lower Britain) in the reign of the Emperor Caracalla (211–17) when Britain, originally a single province, was divided into two. It is also possible, however, that York was selected as a capital because it was already a *colonia*.

The *coloniae* had a dominant role in the politics and administration of their provinces and their essential component was a body of Roman citizens willing to promote the interests of the Roman state. In imperial (as opposed to republican) times a *colonia* was usually created in one of three ways. In the early empire most *coloniae* in, for example, the provinces of Gaul and Spain, were places with an existing population in a settlement of urban character which were promoted on receiving an influx of Roman citizens, usually army veterans or people of Italian origin. In Britain and Germany, which had less sophisticated and more scattered populations at the time of the Roman conquest, *coloniae* were usually created on or adjacent to the sites of Roman military establishments and the bulk of the colonists were made up of veterans. In Britain there were three first-century *coloniae*: at Colchester, Gloucester and Lincoln, which were built directly on the site of fortresses once the legion had moved on. Finally, in the second and third centuries it became common practice in all provinces of the empire to promote towns of low status to the rank of *colonia*, usually to enable them to fulfil some new political function. York has traditionally, if not necessarily correctly, been thought to fall into this third group. In any event, the circumstances of its origins appear to be rather different from those of the other British *coloniae*.

In addition to their legal status, Roman towns were also centres of population, although in Britain they were never able to compete with the great cities of the Mediterranean littoral or even with the larger centres of Gaul and the Rhineland. It is unlikely that any town in Roman Britain had more than 10,000 inhabitants and most probably peaked at about 2–3000. While such a figure represented an unusual concentration of population by British standards of the time, the obvious failure of Roman towns in this country to attract more than a very small proportion of its people serves to fuel the debate on their economic role.

It is arguable that Romano-British towns were principally centres of consumption rather than production since a large proportion of their inhabitants were members of the Roman and native upper class and their retainers, rather than a teeming urban proletariat. The Romano-British towns were, the argument continues, essentially parasitic, sucking in both the fruits of local agriculture and the lion's share of luxury goods imported from abroad, but exported little to their hinterland. The archaeological evidence certainly supports a picture of Romano-British towns as centres for foreign trade, but, at least as far as the first and second centuries are concerned, there is also evidence from York and elsewhere for towns as centres for a wide range of crafts and industries. They presumably formed the basis for some degree of mutually beneficial economic integration of towns and their regions. At the same time, however, the health of the Romano-British urban economy must have been heavily dependent on construction work funded either from the public purse or from the wealth derived from agricultural surplus created by the upper echelons of native society. By the mid-third century these sources of support had begun to dry up and it is apparent that by the end of the fourth century towns were places with a character and role very different from that of their first- and second-century forebears.

In spite of their small size and uncertain economic role, there is no doubt that Romano-British towns had a distinctive appearance which derived from a classical ideal shared with towns throughout the empire. Their most obvious feature was, perhaps, the rectilinear street grid which divided the urban area into *insulae* (literally islands). The central *insulae* were usually occupied by the major public buildings which included the forum, which was a courtyard used as a market or place of public assembly surrounded on three sides by rows of shops or offices. On the fourth side lay the basilica, comparable in form to that of a fortress headquarters building, where government and the administration of justice took place. In *insulae* adjacent to the forum there would usually be a public bath house, temples and, although rare in a British context, a theatre. *Insulae* surrounding these public buildings would have accommodated domestic residences, shops and workshops.

Romano-British town government was also based on an empire-wide model derived from

Rome itself. There was an *ordo*, nominally of 100 men, known as *decuriones*, who were admitted to office on the basis of a property and wealth qualification so that they would be able to pay for public works and festivals. Private, as opposed to public funding was very much the norm in many parts of the empire and towns benefited from the competition between rich men struggling to outdo each other. In Britain, however, private munificence was less common, due, perhaps, to the relative poverty of the native aristocracy or its failure to be impressed with the virtues of urban living. What private funding of construction work we know of, in York and elsewhere, was largely devoted to the construction of temples.

The characteristics of Romano-British towns outlined above, that made them distinct from, as opposed to similar to, their cousins in the Mediterranean heartland of the empire – small size, a fragile economic base and an urban leadership which either lacked funds or Romanized civic values – may be seen as products of the artificial nature of their origins. Roman civilization at the time of the conquest of Britain was based on a governmental system under which the provinces were ruled by town-based elites united by a common culture transmitted by either the Latin or Greek languages. These elites were also united in a common social structure based on the privileges of Roman citizenship. In return for these privileges they collected taxes for the state and rendered military and other public services. The lower orders were kept in check by regular episodes of public generosity which provided food and entertainment – the 'bread and circuses' of Juvenal's memorable phrase.

In Britain the Romans encountered a country without towns and so, in order to govern and tax it, towns had to be created. At the same time, it was hoped that the leaders of native society could be encouraged to live in towns, to take responsibility for their construction, and to assume public office. In the south and east of Britain the progress of town foundation was rapid in the second half of the first century. The sites chosen had usually been occupied by forts or fortresses and were close to, if not on top of, major native settlements. In some cases these settlements, often known as *oppida*, had, as in pre-Roman Gaul, a concentration of population and functions which had brought them close to becoming towns before the conquest.

In the northern and western parts of Britain, however, there were no *oppida*, with the possible exception of Stanwick, and this is probably one reason why urbanization here was rather slower to take off and was ultimately less successful. The pre-Roman tribal groupings in the York area, the Brigantes and Parisi, had had little experience of living in large settled communities. Furthermore, they had relatively little experience of the economic activities such as foreign trade or use of coinage which, up to a point, characterized *oppida* and towns alike. It was not, perhaps, until the early second century that *civitas* capitals were established in the territories of the Brigantes and the Parisi at Aldborough and Brough-on-Humber respectively. Once founded, moreover, these towns did not catch up with those in the south and east of Britain and remained relatively small and poorly furnished with civic amenities. York, as we shall see, was in some senses very different in character, but in others it did suffer from its late start in the race to urbanism.

The civilian settlements at York: north-east of the Ouse

A detailed discussion of evidence for the civilian settlement at York may start on the north-east bank of the Ouse and look in particular at the areas south-east and south-west of the fortress, between the rivers Foss and Ouse (**32**). This is what the Royal Commission referred to as the *canabae*, a term meaning literally booths or stalls and used because it is known to refer to settlements around fortresses elsewhere in the empire. There is no evidence from York, however, that the Romans ever described any part of their settlement here as *canabae* and the status of the area so designated by the Commission remains uncertain.

Little archaeological work has taken place outside the fortress on the north-east bank of the Ouse, although we know of the probable grain warehouse at 39–41 Coney Street (see p.41). In addition, traces of both late first-to second-century timber structures and later Roman stone buildings were excavated at 16–22 Coppergate, the site principally known for its Anglo-Scandinavian discoveries. Other, largely undated, structural remains have been found elsewhere, but not excavated in detail. In the early years of Roman York we may, none the less, imagine a settlement comparable to

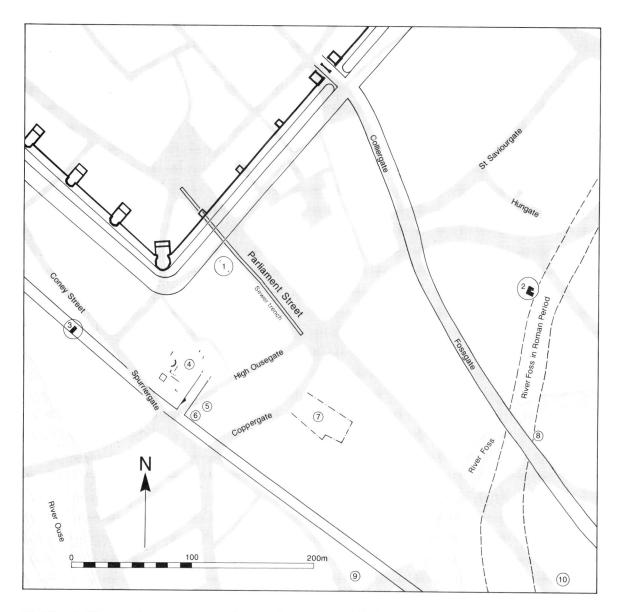

32 *The civilian settlement area south-east of the fortress showing the location of archaeological discoveries, principal excavations and streets (known and conjectured).*

1 *Midland Bank: find spot of altar dedicated to the* Genius Loci *by Quintus Creperius Marcus.*
2 *Garden Place: riverside emplacement.*
3 *39–41 Coney Street: grain warehouse and street*

4 *8 High Ousegate: buildings*
5 *25–7 High Ousegate: buildings*
6 *Find spot of an inscription commemorating the restoration of a temple of Hercules, and another dedicated to the emperors'* numina *and a local goddess.*
7 *16–22 Coppergate: buildings*
8 *Fossgate: possible jetty*
9 *St Mary Castlegate: mosaic*
10 *Tax office Piccadilly: possible jetty*

the so-called *vici* outside the auxiliary forts. These were largely occupied by civilians, but were supervised by the military and served the needs of the army. Adjacent to the east corner of the fortress at York there were, as we have seen (p.43), legionary workshops for tile and pottery manufacture staffed no doubt by some of the local native residents. In addition to quays on the Ouse, supplies for the legion may have passed through others on the banks of a river Foss rather wider than it is today. An emplacement of gritstone blocks found at Garden Place has been interpreted as a possible crane base while a line of stone pillars at the site of the tax office in Piccadilly is thought to have been a jetty.

Although the evidence is sparse, the end of the second century may have been marked by a reorganization of the area south-east and south-west of the fortress and this, in turn, may have accompanied a change of status. The grain warehouse at 39–41 Coney Street was replaced by a gravel street with a fine stone drainage gutter along one side. This street presumably ran along the bank of the river towards the fortress *porta praetoria* and it has also been recorded at a site on the corner of High Ousegate and Spurriergate where it overlay an earlier timber building. The same site revealed a second street which joined the first at an angle of about 90 degrees and probably ran north-eastwards, roughly parallel to the fortress defences. Little is known of buildings around these streets, but parts of substantial stone structures, including a possible bath house, have been observed in the High Ousegate/Spurriergate area.

Other buildings clearly included temples. Inscriptions from a site in Nessgate testify to the existence of one dedicated to Hercules and another dedicated both to a goddess, probably local, whose name begins with the letters IOV, and to the spirits of the emperors (*numinibus augustorum*). These emperors could be Marcus Aurelius and Lucius Verus who ruled jointly from 161 to 169, but they are perhaps more likely to be Septimius Severus and Caracalla. Soldiers presumably played an important part in the cults represented here and another piece of evidence for religious observance in the area was provided by the discovery of an altar in Parliament Street dedicated by Quintus Creperius Marcus to the *Genius Loci* ('the spirit of the place'). This man was probably a soldier,

but the Hercules inscription carries the names of two men, unfortunately incomplete, who clearly had an official connection with an autonomous civilian settlement at York and were, perhaps, members of a college of priests.

In areas to the north-east and north-west of the fortress traces are known of Roman occupation of all periods, but there is nothing to suggest a densely built-up settlement. Much of the land was probably given over to fields and cemeteries (see **57**), but, initially at least, kept clear of buildings to allow the army a clear view of any approaching enemy.

The civilian settlements at York: south-west of the Ouse – origins (33)

For the sake of convenience the civilian settlement on the south-west bank of the Ouse is usually referred to as the *colonia*, although in origin it may have had some other legal title. Strictly speaking, moreover, the extent of the Roman settlement that *colonia* status encompassed is unknown, although the area enclosed by the medieval walls south-west of the Ouse has often been designated as the *colonia* to the exclusion of all others. This appears to be principally because the coffin of a *decurion* of the *colonia*, Flavius Bellator, was recovered from the Roman cemetery adjacent to the walls on the site of the present railway station. It must be considered a distinct possibility, however, that the civilian settlement on the north-east bank of the Ouse received *colonia* status at or about the same time as the settlement on the south-west bank.

On the south-west bank of the Ouse it is reasonable to suggest that the surviving medieval defences define the *colonia* since, for the most part, they probably correspond to and overlie a Roman defensive circuit. York is unusual among medieval towns in having walls sited on top of a pre-existing rampart rather than at ground level. An excavation on the north-east bank of the Ouse near the Anglian Tower has shown that this is because of the existence of the Roman fortress wall and overlying Anglo-Scandinavian and Norman ramparts. By analogy, it is likely that a similar sequence exists on the south-west bank with a *colonia* wall as the earliest feature. It must be admitted, however, that a Roman wall has only been seen in three places beneath the later rampart, all of which were on the north-west side of the enclosure, and in no case in the context of a

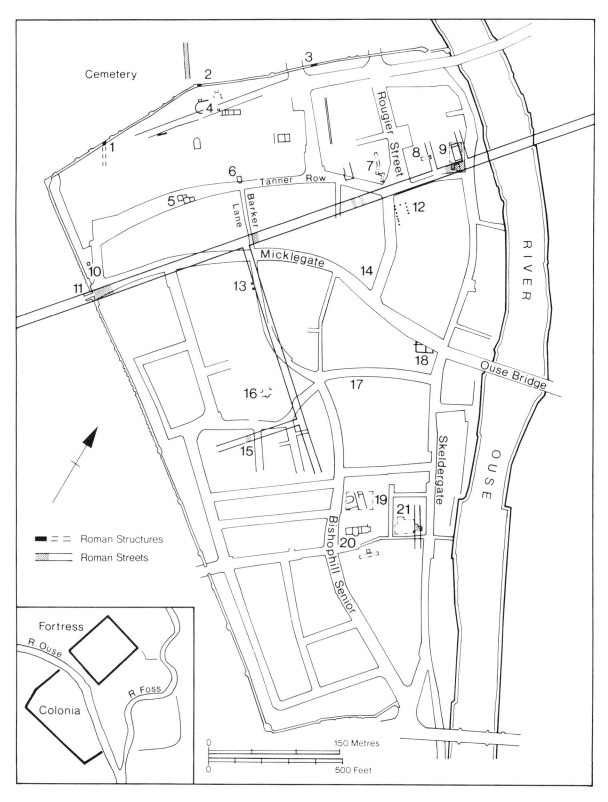

Cemetery

Rougier Street

RIVER

Tanner Row

Barker Lane

Micklegate

Ouse Bridge

Skeldergate

OUSE

Bishophill Senior

Roman Structures

Roman Streets

Fortress

R. Ouse

R. Foss

Colonia

0   150 Metres

0   500 Feet

properly controlled excavation. If one single piece of field-work could be recommended that would be more useful than any other in furthering our knowledge of Roman and indeed post-Roman York, one could do little better than opt for a cross-section through the defences on the south-west bank of the Ouse.

Defences require gates and now that the line of the main road to the south-west has been established it may be suggested that the principal gate to the *colonia* was on or close to the site of medieval Micklegate Bar. This is all the more likely since gate sites are the only feature of Britain's Roman towns, apart from the defensive walls themselves, which regularly survived into the post-Roman period.

There is, of course, no dating for these proposed Roman defences, but it is possible that construction took place at the time of the general move to defend the towns of Roman Britain in the late second century. Alterna-

33 *The civilian settlement on the south-west bank of the Ouse showing the location of archaeological discoveries, principal excavations and streets (known and conjectured).*

1 *Old Station: defences*
2 *Old Station: defences*
3 *Old Station: defences and Mithraic (Arimanius) relief*
4 *Old Station: baths*
5 *Toft Green: mosaics*
6 *Temple of Serapis*
7 *General Accident, Tanner Row: buildings*
8 *5 Rougier Street: warehouse and street*
9 *Wellington Row: main road and building*
10 *Barker Lane: mosaic*
11 *Micklegate Bar*
12 *George Hudson Street: column bases of ?temple or forum basilica*
13 *Trinity Lane: column bases*
14 *Micklegate/George Hudson Street: Mithraic relief and column bases*
15 *Bishophill Junior: street and building*
16 *St Mary Bishophill Junior: house*
17 *Fetter Lane: baths*
18 *Queen's Hotel (1–9 Micklegate): public building*
19 *37 Bishophill Senior: houses and terrace*
20 *St Mary Bishophill Senior: house*
21 *58–9 Skeldergate: street and well.*

tively, the occasion may have been the granting of *colonia* status, an event which was, perhaps, thought to demand the display of architectural splendour which defences provided. Unlike the majority of towns of lower status, the first-century *coloniae* in Britain all had defences, although in the case of Colchester they were not provided at the time of foundation, and at Gloucester and Lincoln they were inherited from the legionary fortresses which had previously occupied the sites. This special treatment may, however, reflect the fact that the erection of defences required the emperor's express permission which was, presumably, most likely to be granted to places with loyal Roman citizens.

As boundaries, rather than as physical protection, Roman town defences also had a strong sacred aspect, serving, for example, to make a symbolic division between the area inhabited by the living within the town and that inhabited by the dead in the cemeteries outside. In addition, defences defined places deemed to be suitable arenas for various important religious functions of an official nature. Many major towns, especially the *coloniae*, incorporated an area dedicated to the local gods in combination with the gods of the Roman state, including the emperor's *numen*, where ceremonial gatherings of provincial leaders took place. At Colchester, for example, there was the temple of the deified Emperor Claudius which was intended to be focus for the imperial cult in Britain. A comparable function may be ascribed to the Altar of the Three Gauls at Condate close to Lyon or the *Ara Ubiorum* (altar of the Ubii people) at the heart of Roman Cologne. Some hint of a comparable role for York is, perhaps, provided by the base of a statue, found near Micklegate Bar, dedicated to the deified province of Britannia by an imperial freedman named Nikomedes. Two emperors are referred to on the inscription and, although their names are not given, the most likely pair are, as on the Nessgate inscription, Septimius Severus and Caracalla.

The importance of the area enclosed by the medieval walls south-west of the Ouse for the study of Roman York became apparent long before it was identified as part of the *colonia*. Ever since the Bishophill altar was found in 1638 there have been frequent discoveries in the area of structures and artefacts during building work, although no systematic archaeological excavation took place here until as recently as 1962 when Peter Wenham excavated

---

the first of a series of small trenches in the Bishophill district. Another small site was excavated by Herman Ramm at St Mary Bishophill Senior in 1964 and one of the York Archaeological Trust's early excavations also took place in Bishophill. While the main Roman road from the south-west was recorded in two small trenches at 27 Tanner Row in 1970, it was not until 1981 that the first thorough investigation of a site in the heart of the Roman town took place, at 5 Rougier Street. Since that year further excavations have confirmed the existence of a well-preserved Roman townscape in this area and at last the mystery surrounding the history and layout of one of Britain's more important Roman towns has begun to clear.

We can only conjecture when the decision was taken to found an urban settlement on the south-west bank of the Ouse, but it is possible that in the late first and early second centuries the area was deliberately kept clear of buildings for military reasons. No buildings and little pottery of the period have been found on any of the sites excavated in recent years, although the Royal Commission suggested that traces of timber structures located north-west of the main Roman road in the area of the Old Station were late first century. It is not entirely clear what the evidence is for this, but the area is one which, on purely topographical grounds, should be considered as a likely focus of early settlement. It is not only close to the road, but occupies high ground commanding a view of the fortress and the Ouse (**34a**).

Unfortunately the archaeology of the Old Station area has been substantially destroyed, but it has produced the very remarkable find of two small bronze plaques dedicated in Greek by a man named Scribonius Demetrius to, in one case, 'the gods of the military commander's residence', and, in the other, to 'Ocean and Tethys', a titan and titaness involved in the Greek creation myth. Demetrius has been identified as a schoolteacher whom the Roman author Plutarch met at Delphi in 83–4 when he heard of the man's experiences on a journey to the 'western isles' beyond the ocean which encircled the civilized world. If these plaques were found close to the place, presumably a temple or shrine, in which they were originally displayed, then they are an important indication of an early Roman presence.

Any area of late first- or early second-century buildings on the north-west side of the later *colonia* enclosure was probably fairly restricted. Firstly because burials of the period have been found inside the walls here; and secondly a legionary cemetery may have existed on land south-east of the main road, if the grave of the ninth legion standard bearer, Lucius Duccius Rufinus, was on the site of Holy Trinity church-yard where his tombstone was found. Similarly, the presence of burials probably allows us to exclude an area in the south-eastern part of the later *colonia* from our search for early occupation. As yet the only possible evidence for an early Roman building south-east of the main road comes from Fetter Lane where part of a bath house, found in 1852, had a room with a floor of ninth legion tiles.

The mid-second century was marked by a radical change in the fortunes of the settlement on the south-west bank of the Ouse. This has, perhaps, been most dramatically revealed by discoveries at the Wellington Row site where we may take up once more the history of the main road from the south-west (**35–36**) (see pp.39–40). Following the early series of gravel surfaces, a surface made of crushed magnesian limestone was laid down. It was cambered on its north-west side, but on its south-east side there was a line of large limestone blocks which served as capping for a trench lined with further blocks and containing a lead pipe of the type used by the Romans for water supply.

These discoveries are of great importance for a number of reasons. First of all, we know that by the fourth century the road was probably double the width that it had been when originally laid out and it is likely that the limestone surface is contemporary with the widening. Although this could not be proved in excavation, the stone-lined pipe trench had probably run down the centre of the road; this conforms to Roman practice elsewhere and is also implied by the fact that the road camber only existed on the north-west side. It can be suggested, therefore, that there would have been another carriageway on the other side of the limestone blocks. This widening, coupled with the establishment of a water supply, would seem to imply a major investment decision and may mark a very significant episode in the history of the area, even, it could be suggested, a deliberate urban foundation.

Whether the road extended at its new width (perhaps *c.* 20 m (65 ft)) with its white surface for more than a short distance from the river

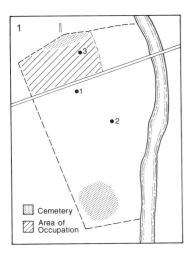 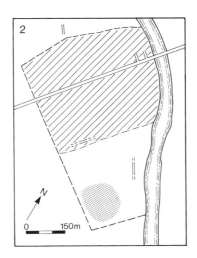 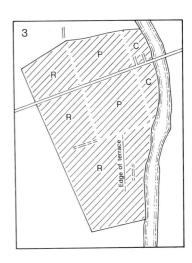

34 *Plans to show how settlement may have developed on the south-west bank of the Ouse:*
1 Late first/early second century: occupation largely confined to the north-west corner.
  1 Find spot of tombstone of Lucius Duccius Rufinus
  2 Fetter Lane bath house
  3 Old Station – find spot of Demetrius' plaques
2 Mid to late second century: expansion into the valley bottom and south-east of the main road to the south-west.
3 Early third century: expansion to the south-east and the area of settlement designated colonia defined by defences.
Key to suggested zone functions:
C Commercial
P Official and public buildings
R Residential

crossing is unknown, but, at all events, when seen from the fortress it must, for a short while at least, have been a fine and dazzling sight.

York – a late second-century boom town
Once the process of settlement had begun on the south-west bank of the Ouse, growth over the next 50–60 years was steady, perhaps even rapid on occasions. The evidence does not, however, support the gradual realization of a single unitary urban plan. Instead it seems likely that there was a series of episodes of expansion, on occasions involving reorganization of areas already colonized, each of which involved the laying out of streets, construction of buildings and carrying out of other public

works such as drainage and terracing. To illustrate an early episode in the sequence we may remain on the Wellington Row site and look at discoveries made in 1988–9 in the largest single area ever excavated archaeologically on the south-west bank of the Ouse (**37**).

One of the earliest features uncovered was a ditch at the north-west end of the site, running towards the river, which may have served both for drainage and as a boundary in some early land division exercise. Another ditch, presumably with similar functions, was found running alongside the main road. These ditches were probably roughly contemporary with a small gravel street running north-west/south-east at 90 degrees to the main road. The life of this layout was brief; the ditches filled up with silt and refuse, and the street was moved a few metres to the north-east to accommodate a stone building. Because its walls, standing in places over 2m (6ft 6in) high, had not, as is usual in York, been comprehensively demolished in later times, and because the interior had not been heavily disturbed by medieval pits, it was possible to trace the building's long and chequered history in some detail.

As originally constructed, the Wellington Row building measured *c.* 15.5 × 10.5m (51ft × 34ft) and lay end-on to the main road (**38**). It overlay the roadside ditch and its south-east wall was founded on the edge of the limestone road surface, although the two were probably constructed at much the same time. The walls were, in contrast to the road, built throughout of oolitic limestone and were founded on footings of clay and cobble strengthened

35 *Mid-second-century limestone surface of the main Roman road from the south-west at Wellington Row. The road runs left to right and the blocks covering the water pipe are at the bottom (1 m scale).*

36 *The lead water pipe in its stone-lined trench at Wellington Row (0.50 m scale).*

with timber piles. The south-east wall continued beyond the south corner to form a wall running along side of the main road. The main door of the building was probably on its north-east side; no entrance was possible on to the main road as the floor level was somewhat lower than the road and any door facing it would have let water in whenever it rained. Equidistant from the walls at the south-east end of the building was a substantial pillar composed of three millstone grit blocks. This must have been the base for a roof support and three other similar pillars had clearly been removed in medieval times as their foundation pits survived. The roof itself was probably composed of thin sandstone slabs which were

found in abundance. As far as the floor is concerned, the south-eastern third of the building, possibly divided from the rest by a partition, had a timber floor of joists with planks over them. Against the south-west wall was an oven made of clay, presumably for cooking or baking.

The oven was, perhaps, the source of a fire which swept through the building early in its life. Evidence for a fire of a similar late second-century date was also found at 5 Rougier Street (see p.77) and it is possible that the whole of the immediate area was affected, although sporadic fires were probably a constant hazard

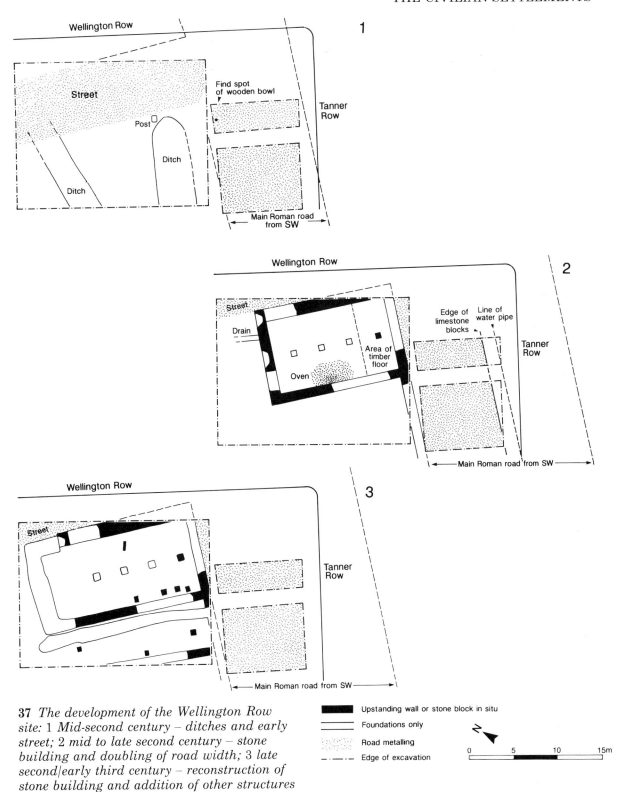

37 *The development of the Wellington Row site: 1 Mid-second century – ditches and early street; 2 mid to late second century – stone building and doubling of road width; 3 late second/early third century – reconstruction of stone building and addition of other structures to the south-west.*

Upstanding wall or stone block in situ

Foundations only

Road metalling

Edge of excavation

0   5   10   15m

38 *Mid-second-century stone building at Wellington Row looking north-west showing* lower left, *the location of joists for the timber floor. The oven was located top left and the original north-west wall is obscured by the shoring brace (2 m scale).*

in York, as in other towns, throughout the Roman period. At all events, damage to the Wellington Row building was considerable and, although the debris had been largely cleared away, some charred floor timbers and joists remained. Most striking of all, the walls had gone a pink or, in places, a bright red colour due to the heat.

After the fire the opportunity was taken in the reconstruction process to extend the building 2 m (6 ft 6 in) to the north-west (**37b** and **colour plate 8**). The upstanding wall of this extension did not survive at all, but a structure of some substance was implied by the construction trench which was 1.5 m (5 ft) deep and packed with clay and cobbles. Driven into

the base were some 200 timber piles, *c.* 3 m (10 ft) long, which were mostly oak logs, but included some reused timbers. At the same time, the floor in the building was levelled up with a thick layer of limestone rubble and mortar. Set on its surface along the south-west wall were four stone blocks (originally there had probably been six) and another longer block was found near the north-east wall. The function of these blocks is unknown, but they are not obviously structural and one possibility is that they served as seats. It may be conjectured that the entrance to the building was now at its north-west end.

Close to the south-west wall of the building and parallel to it there was another slightly later wall, which possibly formed a boundary with the next property to the south-west. Beyond this wall lay a second, apparently associated with a series of stone blocks.

During the excavation it was hoped that some distinctive finds would identify the function of this building about which so much else was known, but in the end all that was reasonably certain was that it was unlikely to have been either a dwelling or a workshop. As we shall see, however, some of the discoveries made in the later fourth-century deposits created the impression that at that time the building had a religious function and this could explain why the plan of the post-reconstruction building had no internal partitions. This suggests a place of assembly, perhaps a temple for the congregation belonging to a religious cult. Alternatively we may be dealing with the meeting place for members of a *collegium* or guild who shared a common occupation, but who also, like their medieval descendants, would have engaged in religious ceremonies.

Some support for this idea of a temple was provided by several small pits dug into the building floor during the third century: in three cases for the burial of pots and in a fourth for a glass bowl. One of the pots had been buried in a wooden box and was found filled with crushed fish bones, possibly the remains of the fish sauce, *garum*, much loved by the Romans. The burial of vessels is, however, not uncommon in Roman buildings and at Wellington Row they presumably represent further examples of the practice, already noted in the fortress, of making offerings to the *genius loci* for the good fortune of a building and its occupants. Buried offerings need not in themselves indicate that a building had a religious function.

Leaving the Wellington Row site for the time being we may return to the main road to look at evidence for what was probably one of the great public works of the later second or early third century. Because it appeared relatively unworn, it seems the limestone surface of the road had a short life before the level was raised by up to 2 m (6 ft 6 in) with layers of cobbles and gravel, creating a causeway standing proud of the contemporary ground surface. This must surely have been done to allow the construction or reconstruction of a bridge across the Ouse. Raising the level on the south-west bank was necessary because of the significantly higher natural level on the north-east bank (**39**). No certain trace of the bridge itself has been found, although substantial stone structures recorded under York's Guildhall may be part of the north-easternmost pier.

Further evidence for rapid development in the mid to late second century was revealed in the 5 Rougier Street trench (**40**). The earliest feature, located at a depth of *c.* 6 m (20 ft) below modern ground level, was a ditch which was aligned on the main road *c.* 5 m (16 ft 6 in) to the south-east. In its final phase of use the ditch was given a timber lining. On the south-east side of the trench there were two stone pillars, in one case made of reused column drums, which had, perhaps, supported the raised floor of a building standing above the ditch which may have served as a drain, being connected to the building by means of a timber-lined chute. It was common practice in Roman times to raise the floors of warehouses off the ground to keep vermin out, allow air to circulate and prevent a build up of dampness. The ditch went out of use when it was cut across by a very substantial wall running north-west/south-east, of which a base course of massive millstone grit blocks survived. Both the wall and pillars were succeeded by a thick dump of burnt material composed largely of grain, but also including charred timber. This material probably resulted from the collapse of the warehouse during a fire.

As at Wellington Row, there was reconstruction after the fire and this evidently involved an element of replanning in the immediate neighbourhood. The gritstone wall was replaced by a gravel street running north-west/south-east at 90 degrees to the main road. South-west of the street a new warehouse was probably constructed with a floor again raised on stone pillars (**41**). If the identification of these remains is correct, this building and its predecessor may be testimony to York's importance as a centre for the collection and marketing of agricultural products in the late second and early third centuries. Of some interest in this context was the discovery in the burnt deposit of part of a small stone relief depicting a cockerel bearing little bags on its back (**42**). Above the bird is a pair of feet which probably belonged to a representation of Mercury who is frequently accompanied by a cockerel in Romano-British art. One of Mercury's functions was to protect traders, but he was also the messenger of the gods and the messages themselves may have been symbolically contained in the cockerel's bags.

Commercial and craft activities

Evidence for commercial activities and, in addition, the crafts practised in late second-century York came from the nearby General Accident Extension site in Tanner Row

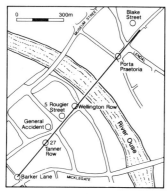

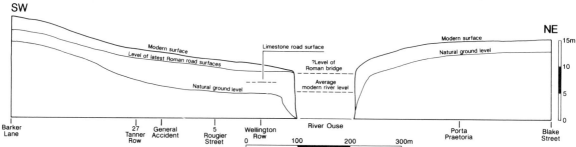

39 *Simplified cross-section across York (with location plan) from Barker Lane (south-west) to Blake Street (north-east) along the line of the main Roman road from the south-west showing relative ground levels on opposite banks of the Ouse.*

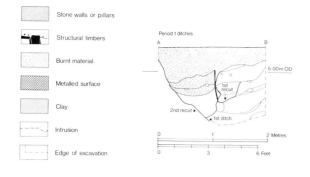

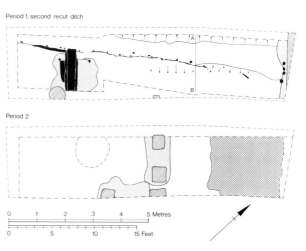

40 *5 Rougier Street – sequence of development in the late second and early third century. Top: cross-section through mid- to late-second century ditch. Period 1: timber-lined ditch fed by chute (left). Period 2: Street running north-west/south-east (right) and stone pillars.*

41 *5 Rougier Street – stone pillars which probably supported a warehouse facing the street which ran left to right beyond the 1 m-scale (late second century).*

(General Accident for short). The earliest archaeological feature was a continuation of the ditch found at 5 Rougier Street. Roughly contemporary with its use, probably in the 160s or 170s, there was an episode of ground preparation which involved building up the level at the south-east end of the site with layers of turf and clay. This compensated for the gentle natural slope rising from south-east to north-west and created two level platforms, divided by a low revetment, suitable for building.

Parts of two timber buildings were found (**43–44**), although it was not possible to get complete

42 *Relief of a cockerel, probably symbolizing Mercury, on a block of magnesian limestone from 5 Rougier Street.*

79

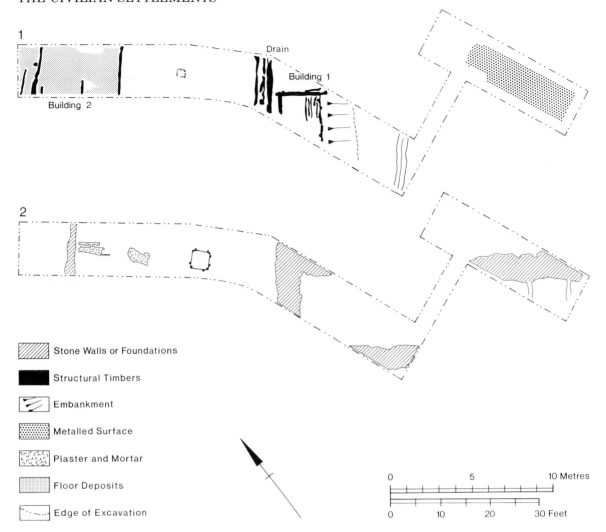

Stone Walls or Foundations

Structural Timbers

Embankment

Metalled Surface

Plaster and Mortar

Floor Deposits

Edge of Excavation

0   5   10 Metres

0   10   20   30 Feet

43 *General Accident, Tanner Row – sequence of development in the late second and early third century:* 1 *Timber buildings, ditch* (centre right) *and cobbled surface* (right). 2 *Stone building.*

plans of them because of the narrowness of the trenches. Little upstanding wall survived as demolition later in the Roman period had been thorough, but it was clear that Building 1, nearest the main road, had been constructed with walls based on sill beams held in position by posts. These posts had also projected upwards and had horizontal planks nailed to them. There was probably a timber plank floor. Immediately to the north-west there was a large timber-lined drain which had been used for the disposal of kitchen waste and human faeces, the presence of the latter being betrayed by large quantities of the eggs of parasitic worms which live in the gut. To the north-west of the drain Building 2 was found. Its remains were fewer, but the bases of two walls survived as timber sill beams resting on layers of clay and stones. Completing the contemporary layout at the south-east end of the site, beyond the ditch, was a spread of cobbles probably representing a yard alongside the main road. It appears that horses or cattle were coralled or stabled in this area as the overlying layer consisted largely of hay-rich dung. At some stage in the late second century Buildings 1 and 2 were reconstructed and one wall in Building 1 was given a form of 'cavity wall' with planks nailed on to both sides of the upright posts (**45**).

1 Tombstone of the ninth legion standard bearer Lucius Duccius Rufinus.

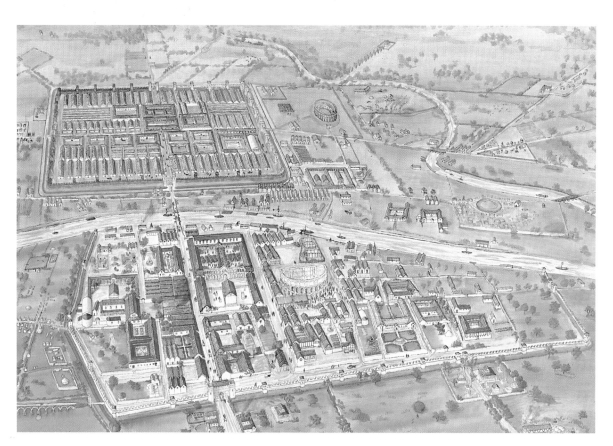

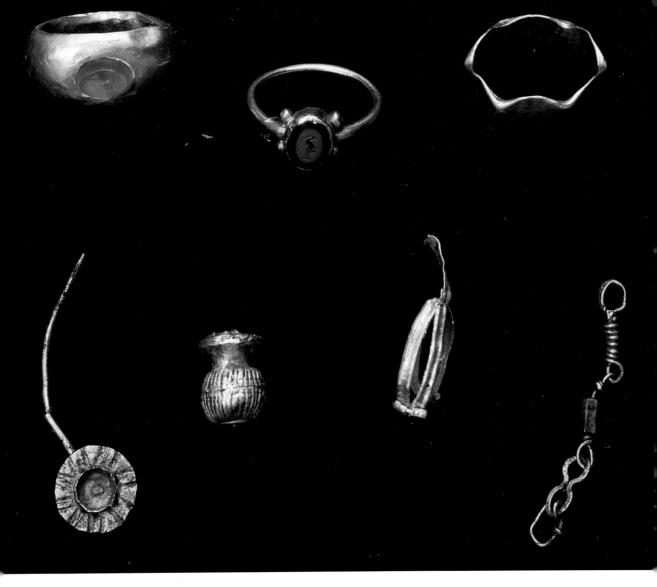

4 Roman gold jewellery from York. *Top row:* Rings; *bottom row:* ear-ring, pendant fitting, ear-ring and pendant chain (middle two from the Church Street sewer).

2 *Top left:* Conjectural reconstruction of York at the time of the visit of Septimius Severus in 209-11 viewed from the south-west. The fortress is in the background and the *colonia* south-west of the Ouse is in the foreground. (Tracey Croft.)

3 *Bottom left:* Aerial view of York today from the south-west.

5 Pottery vessels in 'Ebor Ware' manufactured in a tradition begun by the army, but later adopted by civilians.

6 Fragment of a green-glazed double-handled cup with relief satyrs from the Wellington Row site, probably first century.

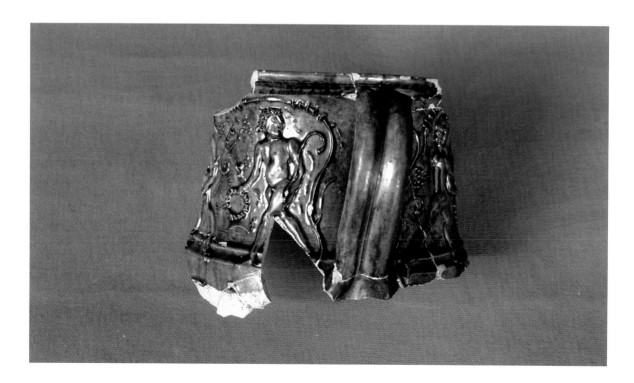

7 Wall plaster from a room added to the north-west side of the basilica of the fortress *principia* in the fourth century, now on display near its find spot in York Minster Foundations.

8 Wellington Row – the stone building as reconstructed after the fire with a limestone and mortar floor surface and stone blocks along the walls. The surviving roof support pillar is at the south-east end of the building to the right of the picture (2m scale).

9 The Multangular Tower at the west corner of the legionary fortress.

10 A reconstruction drawing of the building of Interval Tower SW5.

11 A bust in magnesian limestone thought to be of the Emperor Constantine I (height: 45cm) (18in).

12 Detail of the Four Seasons mosaic from Toft Green showing 'Spring'.

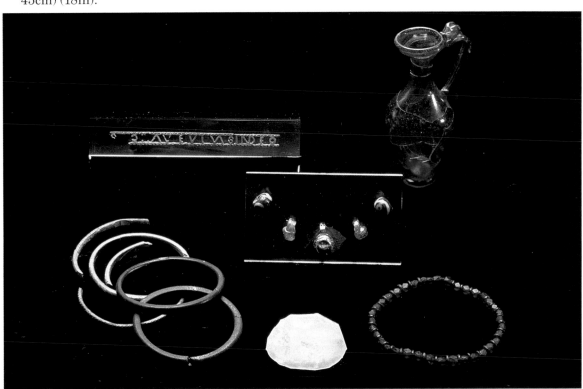

13 A fourth-century grave group including a small bone plaque with an openwork inscription SOROR AVE VIVAS IN DEO thought to be Christian in sentiment. In addition there are two jet bangles, a bracelet of blue glass beads, silver and bronze lockets, two yellow glass ear-rings, two marbled glass beads and a small round glass mirror.

44 *Late second-century timber buildings at the General Accident, Tanner Row site (1 m scale). The north-east end wall of Building 1 runs diagonally from lower left towards the centre of the picture where it meets a timber-lined drain.*

In the layers around the General Accident buildings there was abundant evidence for craft activity, especially metalworking. Slag from iron smithing and copperworking occurred in some quantity, along with numerous iron offcuts and iron tools. Leatherworking is attested by large quantities of offcuts and shoe fragments (**46**). In addition, the complete panel of an army tent and scraps of others were found. On one of these scraps careful cleaning by the conservators revealed a graffito scratched into the leather which refers to the Century of Sollius Julianus. This man has been identified with Marcus Sollius Julianus named on a building stone on Hadrian's Wall commemorating a stretch of the wall built by his men. We have, therefore, a remarkable testimony to the connection between the sixth legion on the wall and its base in York. Other military equipment from around the General Accident buildings included a pattern-welded sword, possibly brought to the site for repair or recycling, and several fittings from military equipment. In short, the evidence is that in the latter part of the second century this part of York was occupied by people engaged in a variety of crafts and a major source of their income may have come from services to the military. The prosperity that metalworking could sometimes bring is suggested by the fine tombstone found at Dringhouses *c.* 2.5 km ($1\frac{1}{2}$ miles) south-west of the *colonia* which shows a smith at work (**47**).

45 *Detail of the post and plank wall of Building 1 at the General Accident, Tanner Row site.*

The diet of the inhabitants

In addition to evidence for crafts, the late second-century deposits at General Accident also produced large quantities of food remains which give an insight into the diet of the period and also into aspects of Roman York's trading contacts. Research by Terry O'Connor of the Environmental Archaeology Unit has shown that the principal source of meat was beef, supplemented by a little mutton and pork. Of particular interest, however, was the evidence for a butchery in the area, which had probably produced meat products on a commercial scale. The evidence takes the form, firstly, of smashed up cattle limb bones, the residue of systematic marrow extraction. Secondly, there were large numbers of beef scapulae interpreted as remains from the smoking of 'boned out' shoulders of beef. O'Connor has suggested this meat was something of a luxury given the expense consequent on the time and labour involved in its preparation.

The bones themselves, especially the horns, suggest that there were two breeds of cattle. One was the so-called 'Celtic short-horn' (**48**) with small, tightly curved horns, markedly oval in cross-section. The other had larger and less tightly curved horns and it is possible that this represents an introduction of the Roman period. In both cases, however, the beasts were small compared to our own cattle and were essentially multi-purpose, being used for milk and haulage as well as meat. This may explain the relative absence of young animals under three years old. Cattle were also valued for their hide and one may envisage a close relationship between the local butchers and leatherworkers.

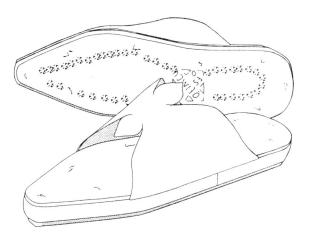

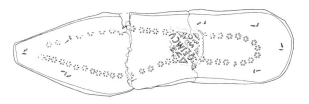

46 *Sole of a sandal with maker's mark stamped on it from the General Accident site, Tanner Row. At the top is a reconstruction of the sandal.*

47 *Tombstone of a smith found at Dringhouses in 1860.*

A staple in the Romans' diet was bread together with other dishes with a cereal content. It is appropriate, therefore, that Roman York has produced large quantities of cereal grain, two deposits being of particular importance. The charred grain from the 39–41 Coney Street warehouse consisted, firstly, of about 60 per cent spelt wheat, the principal crop of the Roman period which can be distinguished from bread wheat by having grains which are not so easily removed from the ears. Secondly, about 25 per cent of the deposit was barley and about 15 per cent rye. The grain from the burnt dump at 5 Rougier Street consisted of around 89 per cent spelt wheat and about 11 per cent barley. The barley was probably used for animal feed or brewing and the rye may also have been used to produce alcoholic beverages. Both deposits contained the seeds of a number of field weeds. Their diversity indicates that in the late second

century York drew its grain from a variety of ecological zones, some of which were 20 km (12 miles) and more distant. The impact of the Roman town on the agricultural economy of its surrounding region in respect of cereal production alone must, therefore, have been considerable. One weed whose seeds are of particular interest is the corncockle. This has a fine pink flower and was common in British fields before the regular use of selective weed-killers. The seeds are, however, poisonous and if incorporated in cereal-based foods would have caused a serious Roman stomach ache!

In addition to locally-produced foodstuffs, General Accident produced small amounts of

48 *Horns of a cow of 'Celtic short-horn type' from General Accident, Tanner Row (max. width 290 mm (11½ in)).*

material imported from further afield including crabs, perhaps from Bridlington Bay on the Yorkshire coast, and herring which were probably caught in the Humber estuary. From beyond Britain came olives, grapes and figs. Wine does not, of course survive, but numerous sherds of wine amphorae from all sites in the *colonia* confirm that it was as popular with the civilians as with the soldiers. Finally, there were the bones of a breed of dormouse native to Gaul which, while not the classic edible type mentioned in literary sources, may have been an acceptable substitute (see **51a**). Although small in quantity, the evidence for non-local food, along with the smoked beef, is important as it suggests the presence of a community in which there were people who not only had sophisticated tastes, but also the wealth to gratify them. In this sense the food remains alone indicate that by the end of the second century the Roman civilian settlement at York had acquired a distinct character and status.

Trading contacts
Roman York presumably attracted many other goods besides foodstuffs, but in the majority of cases they would have been made of perishable materials which do not survive. There were, however, a few non-perishable imports; these included building materials, especially stone (see pp.40–1). A commodity which survives well and can give some indication of the direction,

if not the quantity, of both interregional and overseas trade is pottery. As far as wares of continental origin are concerned, the late second century is the heyday of samian ware imports to York. For the most part they come from central Gaul with a source at a workshop at Lezoux near Clermont Ferrand being particularly important, but there is a smaller amount from eastern Gaulish workshops centred on Trier. The Rhineland, principally Cologne, was also the source of what are usually known as 'colour-coated' beakers and jars which have low relief decoration and a shiny purple finish.

Further evidence for links with the Rhineland is provided by another component of York's trade, in this case an export. Jet is a mineral akin to coal which is found on the north-east coast of Yorkshire in the Whitby area. It can be easily cut and given a high polish. Static electricity is generated when jet is rubbed and this gave it an aura of magic in antiquity. Jet does occur in other parts of Europe, but much of the Roman material found in the western empire probably came from Britain. While jet may have been shipped raw, it is also clear that there were workshops in York which exported finished pieces (**49**). Among the commoner jet items were beads, bracelets, hair pins and rings, but more elaborate pieces include medallion pendants bearing human portraits and, most striking of all, gorgon masks which served to repel the evil eye.

The archaeological evidence suggests that York's trading contacts, especially over long distances, were at their most extensive in the

49 *Jet objects from Roman York. The medallions depict* (from left to right) *a betrothed couple, a gorgon mask and a family group.*

late second and early third centuries when the economic and political conditions in the western empire still favoured the activities of sea-going merchants. We know the names of a small number of these men from inscriptions and they include Lucius Viducius Placidus, referred to as a *negotiator* (merchant) on an inscription dated to 221 found in excavations at Clementhorpe (**50**). This is a rare British example of the commemoration of building work by a private individual, in this case an arch and vaulted passage which may, perhaps, have formed part of a temple complex. The inscription also tells us that Placidus came from the territory of the Veliocasses centred on what is now Rouen in northern Gaul. It is likely that our man gained his citizenship during the reign of Caracalla as he is known without the *tria nomina*, simply as Placidus son of Viducus, on an inscription dredged from the Rhine estuary in the Netherlands. In typical native fashion he Romanized his father's name to form the *nomen gentilicium* Viducius and Placidus was kept as a *cognomen*. One can speculate that his success in the world was based largely on trade across the North Sea, involving, perhaps, the carriage of wine and pottery from Cologne or Trier to York and

return trips with agricultural products and jet jewellery.

While the evidence for trade in York of the late second and early third centuries is considerable, we do not as yet know where the all-important river quays lay. If the evidence from London is anything to go by, however, there were major waterfront structures somewhere on the banks of the river Ouse where ships plying both coastal and overseas trade would load and unload. It is most likely, perhaps, that larger vessels berthed downstream from the bridge, adjacent to what are now North Street and Skeldergate.

Environmental evidence

In addition to providing evidence for the consumption and marketing of foodstuffs, the organic matter preserved on the General Accident site is of interest for illustrating the ecological history of the *colonia*. It is clear that over a period of about 50 years, there was a radical change from an environment subject to little human influence, beyond, perhaps, the grazing of stock, to one bearing the imprint of permanent settlement. The most striking witness to this was the increasing occurrence of decomposing organic matter which became abundant around the buildings. It probably derived from a number of sources, including food remains, human and animal faeces, and the litter from floor-covering and bedding. There was also cereal debris and hay, which

50 *Stone tablet dated 221 commemorating the construction of an arch and passage – (A)RCUM ET IANUM – by the merchant – (N)EGOTIATOR – Lucius Viducius Placidus from the territory of the Veliocasses (centred on Rouen). Found at Clementhorpe in 1976.*

must have come from the stabling of horses.

The somewhat squalid environs of the building provided ideal habitats for a diverse fauna which enjoyed the company of man, if not vice versa. An enormous variety of insects included house flies and stable flies, fleas and any number of dung beetles and species suited to life in damp timber buildings. From the occurrence of their bones we may imagine that rodents such as house mice and rats were very common.

Rather than the brown variety common today, however, the rats would have been the black *Rattus rattus* (**51b**). Its fleas are thought to have carried bubonic plague, most notoriously as the medieval Black Death, but the disease may also have been a hazard in Roman times.

Disease-ridden or not, the ecological evidence does cast a rather new light on the conditions which might, on occasions, prevail in Roman towns, traditionally thought to have been models of order and cleanliness. It is difficult to know, however, if the evidence from General Accident is any way typical as waterlogged conditions are so rare. Even in a York context it is possible that the squalor was purely localized and a product of the refuse tipping habits of a restricted section of the community.

51 *Rodents of Roman York:* a *the garden dormouse* (Eliomys quercinus) *with the edible dormouse* (Glis glis) *shown (top) for comparison;* b *the black rat* (Rattus rattus)

The public buildings

One indication that environmental conditions at General Accident in the late second century were unusual and, in due course, considered by the authorities to be undesirable is that in the early third century there was a marked change in the character of occupation on the site. The timber buildings were deliberately demolished and there was then an episode of levelling-up prior to the construction of a considerable stone structure. Its walls had, unfortunately, been completely robbed and its floors greatly disturbed by post-Roman robbing, but the substantial nature of the foundations suggests that this was a major public building. It may even have been part of the same structure as that recorded as having a substantial 'gritstone facade' which was found a little to the south-west of the General Accident site in 1901. One reason for the new arrangements may be that the manufacturing activities hitherto practised here were now considered unduly dangerous or noisome and were moved to some less central location, but the change may also be to do with the town's acquisition of the status of *colonia* and provincial capital.

The location of the forum of *Eboracum*, the centre of its civic life, is unknown, although it was probably close to the main road to the south-west. One possible location lies almost opposite the General Accident site where column bases in two rows 12 m (40 ft) apart were recorded in 1898. One row had seven bases and the other four and in each case they were 1.80 m (6 ft) apart; an intermediate column stood on the side facing the road. It is possible that these columns belonged to a temple of classical style, but it is equally likely that they stood in the forum basilica. This latter notion acquires some support from the discovery of an altar dedicated to the spirit of the emperor linked to that of the *genius* of *Eboracum* nearby in George Hudson Street. Shrines to the emperor were frequently located in the *aedes* of civilian fora just as they were in those of fortress headquarters buildings.

The cult was serviced by the *seviri augustales* (literally the six men of the emperor), usually wealthy freedmen who nominally owed their freedom to their ultimate master, the emperor, and often took his name. We know of two *seviri* from York, one of whom was Marcus Aurelius Lunaris and the other was Verecundius Diogenes. The latter's coffin is now lost, but surviving illustrations show an inscription giving his place of origin as what is now Bourges in southeast France. Remarkably, the coffin of his wife is also known and its inscription names her as Julia Fortunata from Sardinia. The pair epitomize the cosmopolitan nature of the upper classes of the Roman *colonia* at York at the peak of its prosperity and self-confidence when it must have seemed on the verge of becoming another of the empire's great cities.

Another site in the centre of the *colonia* which has produced substantial building remains is the Queen's Hotel site (1–9 Micklegate) which was excavated in 1988–9. Unfortunately due to problems of access and funding, full excavation in advance of redevelopment was not possible and only a fraction of the Roman building remains on the site were examined in detail. It is evident, however, that in the early third century an extensive stone structure, of unknown function, succeeded the usual mid to late second-century episode of ditch digging and rubbish dumping (see **61**). The building had been sturdily founded on massive stone footings 2.5 m (8 ft) deep, employing the pitched limestone slab technique. No superstructure survived as it had been demolished when a second and even more substantial building was erected later in the third century. Its spectacular remains will be described in the next chapter.

The third area to produce public buildings takes us back to the north-western part of the *colonia* where structural remains have been found indicating the presence of an extensive baths complex. Unfortunately, little detail is known as they were unearthed during the construction of the Old Station in 1839 and of a bomb shelter a century later, in 1939. There were clearly two or more phases of building. The first consisted of relatively small structures, including three cold plunge baths, which, if correctly recorded, apparently lay on an alignment slightly different to that of the main road from the south-west, but possibly conforming to the line of a minor road approaching the area from the north-west. Of a later date, and more nearly on the main road alignment, was an apsed *caldarium* 9 m (30 ft) wide and at least 10.5 m (34 ft) long which for sheer size is almost unparalleled in Britain. Other discoveries in this area indicate the presence of temples to the gods Serapis and Mithras.

It is difficult to know how to interpret these discoveries, but we may be dealing with the public baths of *Eboracum* and an associated area of public assembly dedicated to a variety of social functions, including religious observance. A comparable enclave, set apart from residential and commercial areas, has been identified in the south-western part of Roman London. It is even possible that it is in this area of high ground, somewhat apart from the centre of the town, that the palace of the provincial governor of Lower Britain should be looked for, although it should be remembered that until the reforms of the later third century, separating military and political functions, this post was held by the legionary legate who probably continued to live in the fortress.

It is clear that the religious practices of the townspeople were as diverse as those of the soldiers and it is of particular interest that York, like other Roman towns, was a centre for the new religious cults which, as a result of the movement of soldiers and merchants, swept through the empire from the east in the second and third centuries. These 'mystery cults' as they are sometimes known were rather different in character to the native British and official Roman cults as they were based on a theology offering believers a more intimate relationship with the deity and, at the same time, access to the secret knowledge which would guarantee spiritual renewal and eternal life. Admittance to the congregation of believers usually required an initiation rite of some kind which might range from forms of baptism to unpleasant physical ordeals.

Mystery cults practised in York evidently included the worship of Isis, Cybele and Mithras. A centre for the first of these would have been a small building south-east of the baths which, from the fine dedicatory inscription (see 2), is known to have been associated with the worship of Serapis, one of the deities in the cult. The central figure in the cult was the goddess herself who suckled a baby son, Harpokrates. On achieving manhood Harpokrates avenged the death of his father, Serapis, who had been killed by the evil god Seth. Serapis was then restored to life by Isis. This idea of death and rebirth is comparable to that involved in the cult of Cybele, a mother goddess with fertility powers. Part of the Cybele myth was the story of Atys, probably depicted on a fragment of a tomb monument found on The Mount. He was Cybele's paramour who castrated himself in remorse for his infidelity and priests of the cult were themselves eunuchs.

Mithraism concerned itself with a spiritual journey from the darkness of death to the light of everlasting life. The central myth of Mithraism involved the sacrifice of a great bull which had been created at the beginning of time. This sacrifice is known as the *tauroctony* and can be seen on the Mithraic relief found on Micklegate (see 2), which suggests the presence of a temple in the heart of the *colonia*. From the blood of the bull came all life and so an apparent act of destruction was transformed into one of creation. Mithras, the lord of light, was set in opposition to the evil god Arimanius (52), whose placation would have inspired the altar from York found on the defences near the Old Railway Station. This, the only representation of Arimanius known from this country, depicts him as a winged figure, naked except for a fringed loin cloth tied with a knotted snake symbolizing the tortuous course of both the sun through the sky and of the initiate to revelation. He also carries a sceptre to

52 *Statue of Arimanius, the devil in Mithraic mythology, dedicated by Volusius Ireneus who paid his vow willingly and deservedly –* V(OTUM) [S(OLVENS) L(IBENS) M(ERITO).

symbolize his power, along with the keys of heaven.

Houses and homes

It is entirely appropriate that the altar from Bishophill should refer to the 'gods of hospitality and home' as it was found in the principal residential zone of the *colonia* south-east of the public buildings. The earliest activity in this area appears to date to the mid to late second century when a street, excavated at 58–9 Skeldergate, was established close to the riverfront. Another street of similar date was located at Bishophill Junior running north-east/south-west, probably parallel to the main road to the south-west. It is possible, however, that the area south-east of this street was not as yet densely settled (see **34b**) and archaeological evidence of the period is confined to a small metalworking structure at St Mary Bishophill

Senior. At the 37 Bishophill Senior and Bishophill Junior sites there was a charcoal-rich deposit which suggests ground clearance by some sort of 'slash and burn' procedure. The major change to the topography of the area took place in the early third century (see **34c**) when the naturally steep-sloping valley side was terraced by building outwards from the higher ground to create a level platform for buildings. The full extent of the terrace is uncertain, but it may have been 2–300 m (660–980 ft) in length and was clearly a massive undertaking requiring thousands of tons of material and considerable labour to construct.

Extensive, but heavily robbed, remains of stone buildings on the terrace have been found at 37 Bishophill Senior and St Mary Bishophill Senior which were presumably domestic residences of some pretension. There was evidence for apsed *triclinia* (dining rooms), underfloor heating, decorative wall plaster and marble veneers. Fragmentary remains of other buildings have been found at the Bishophill Junior site and in watching briefs on Bishophill Senior. As yet, however, the density of occupation remains unknown and it is not possible to be confident that the *colonia* ever had a population of a size to match its status.

One further question regarding the topography of the *colonia* which should be addressed at this point is how access to the south-eastern zone was achieved. One route clearly ran along the riverside, but in addition, another route may have joined the main road to the south-west at right angles after running along level ground at the top of the slope which rises up from the river. Over much of its course this route would have corresponded to the south-west edge of the terrace. Buildings on the 37 Bishophill Senior and St Mary Bishophill Junior sites (although not St Mary Bishophill Senior) respect the north-east/south-west alignment of the main road implying the continuation of a street grid based on it. A street on the suggested line may also be indicated by the location of two column bases, perhaps from a roadside colonnade, found in Trinity Lane.

Civilized living in the Roman houses on Bishophill would have depended on a ready water supply. The Wellington Row site has already demonstrated that some parts of Roman York had piped water and further evidence for this takes the form of a remarkable stone fountain found in Bishophill Junior in 1906

(53). It consists of a tank *c.* 1.15 m (3 ft 9 in) square and *c.* 1 m (3 ft) high made of slabs of magnesian limestone bound with iron straps. The back slab rises a further 22 cm (8 in) and is pierced by an inlet which would have been connected to the public supply. As in the fortress the source of the water is unknown, but it is possible that an aqueduct brought a supply from the south-west to a distribution centre on the high ground in the baths area. Piped water would have been supplemented by wells and a very fine timber-lined example some 6 m (20 ft) deep was excavated at 58–9 Skeldergate (54).

The people of the town

The inhabitants of this agreeable south-eastern part of the *colonia* offering pleasant views over the Ouse and a retreat from the bustle, noise and smells of the public buildings and quayside, are, of course, largely unknown to us as individuals. We may imagine, however, that numbered amongst the more prosperous were some of those people whose names have survived on funerary monuments. As already seen, they included civic officials, legionary veterans, and merchants, but these men also had families and York is remarkable for the number of inscriptions which refer to women and children. One of the finest tombstones is that of Julia Velva which shows a splendid family dining scene (see back cover). Adopting a pose commonly depicted on Roman tombstones the lady herself reclines on a couch in a semi-circular apsed recess which no doubt recalled the *triclinia* of the smarter town houses. In the Roman world it was considered the height of good manners to dine while reclining; only servants and children sat at table. To one side of Julia Velva's couch stands a booted male figure, presumably her husband Aurelius Mercurialis who had her tombstone set up. To the left there are two children; a girl is seated holding a pet bird and a boy is standing. Between them is a table set with dishes of food which presumably symbolize a funeral banquet.

Another insight into life in Roman York is provided by the coffin of Aelia Severa, relict of Caecilius Rufus (55). She is referred to as a member of the *honestiores* and this serves to make the point that even after Caracalla's extension of citizenship Roman society remained as hierarchical as ever. The *honestiores* formed the upper crust occupying positions

53 *The stone street fountain from Bishophill Junior.*

of importance in government and administration, and enjoying wide-ranging privileges, while the mass of the population, known as the *humiliores*, remained very much second-class citizens. Aelia Severa's coffin also tells us that it was paid for by Caecilius Musicus, a *libertus* or freed slave, who had evidently taken his master's *nomen* on receiving manumission and we might guess from his *cognomen* that his previous job had been as household musician.

An impression of the appearance of Roman women in York can be gained from their tombstones, including those of Julia Brica (56) and Candida Barita which show them dressed in the long cloaks typical of the time. Their names suggest that they were native Britons and it is possible that they were married to legionary veterans who had found them as attractive as a girl named Claudia Rufina encountered in Rome by the poet Martial who wrote:

Though brought up among the sky-blue Britons,
She has the spirit of the latin race

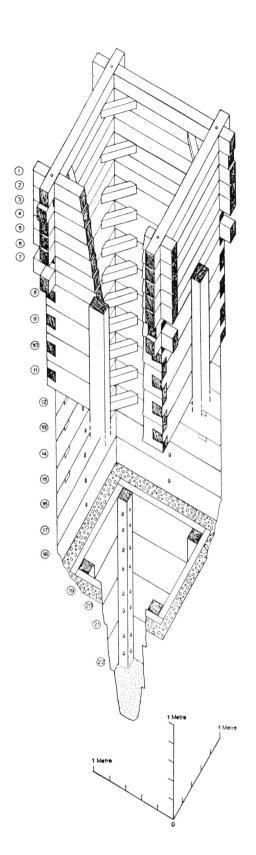

Julia Brica is recorded as dying at the age of
31 and her child Sempronia Martina at the age
of six. In an era of little medical knowledge
infant mortality was high, and sad testimony
to this is also provided by Candida Barita's
tombstone which records that she was accompanied to the 'divine shades' by her two little
daughters Mantia and Tetrica. The most touch-
ing testimony to the devotion of local people
to their families is, however, the tombstone of
little Corellia Optata who was mourned by her
father as follows:

> To the spirits of the departed. Corellia
> Optata, 13 years old. Ye hidden spirits, that
> dwell in Pluto's Acherusian realms, whom
> the scanty ash and the shade, the body's
> image, seek after life's little day, I, the
> pitiable father of an innocent daughter,
> caught by cheating hope, lament her final
> end. Quintus Corellius Fortis, the father had
> this made.

The cemeteries
According to Roman law the dead had to be
buried outside areas inhabited by the living.
Typically, therefore, cemeteries lined the main
roads as they approached settlements, so that
passers-by could pay due respect to the dead
and keep their memory green.

With the exception of the Trentholme Drive
site, where Peter Wenham found 53 cremation
graves and some 342 inhumations (i.e. graves
where the body was buried unburnt) dating
from the mid-second to early fourth century,
the known Roman cemeteries of York were
largely unearthed in the nineteenth century. It
is difficult, therefore, to understand both their
overall development and the details of burial
practice. It is clear, however, that on the north-
east bank of the Ouse major cemeteries existed
on the roads to the north-west in the Bootham
area and on the road to the south-east in the
Fishergate area. On the south-west bank the
cemeteries were concentrated to the north-west

54 *The timber-lined well from 58–9 Skeldergate, an axonometric reconstruction. Tiers 1–7
saddle jointed, excluding tier 6 (half-lap), with
corner braces and external retaining posts;
tiers 8–18 dovetail jointed, 16–18 without
braces; tiers 19–22 inset with internal corner
posts.*

91

55 *The coffin of Aelia Severa, a lady of the upper classes, the* honestiores – HONESTE FEMINE – *once the wife of Caecilius Rufus, who lived 27 years, 9 months, 4 days –* V(IXIT) AN(NOS) XXVII M(ENSES) VIII D(IES) IIII. *The coffin was set up by Caecilius Musicus, freedman –* LIB(ERTUS). *Found in 1859 in Dalton Terrace.*

of the defences and along the main road to the south-west, but burials have also been found to the south-east, some of which were in an area which by the early third century had probably been incorporated into the town.

Evidence from Roman towns elsewhere suggests that, at least until the later fourth century, York's cemeteries would have expanded outwards from the settlement boundaries. Within cemeteries there would have been distinct plots owned by families or occupational and other social groups. The rich and powerful usually strove to secure plots in prominent locations close to the roads, not only for pious reasons, but also to remind visitors and locals alike of who the most important people in the community were. It is no surprise, therefore, that at York many of the sculpted funerary monuments come from areas close to the minor road which approaches the *colonia* from the north-west and either side of the main road from the south-west as it rises up what is now The Mount. One of the reasons for suggesting that the Trentholme Drive cemetery contained the humbler members of the community is its location at the bottom of the hill in marshy ground close to what is still known as the Knavesmire.

The York evidence suggests a great variety of burial practice, as would be expected in a place which was home to people of diverse geographical origins whose status in society ranged from the highest ranks of the Roman government and military establishments to the humblest of slaves.

The earliest burials were usually cremations which involved burning the body and then interring the remains in some sort of vessel, either of pottery, glass or lead. At Trentholme Drive a stone structure surrounded by a dense layer of charcoal was interpreted as the site where the cremation process itself took place. Cremation fell out of favour in the second century to be replaced by inhumation. The graves were usually simple bath-shaped pits, but the bodies were frequently interred in wooden coffins. Lead and stone coffins are decorated with sculptures and containing a subterranean vault such as that which still survives at 104 The Mount. Remains of a more modest version, probably of early third-century date, stood on a site recently excavated at 35–41 Blossom Street. Although largely demolished in later Roman times, it had measured 6 × 6 m (20 × 20 ft), with stone walls plastered on the inside and an *opus signinum* floor. An adult female had been buried on a north-east/south-west alignment within the mausoleum. Subsequently, other burials with a similar orientation were made nearby. More humble memorials must have existed, although another reason for identifying Trentholme Drive as a cemetery of the poorer classes was its apparent lack of grave markers. This may have contributed to a marked lack of order as graves lay on a variety of alignments and frequently cut into one another.

In at least some cases bodies were buried clothed, although all that usually survives are jewellery items, such as rings and bracelets, and occasionally the iron hobnails of boots and shoes. Votive offerings were frequently included in graves of all types, with pottery vessels the most common items. Originally they may have contained foodstuffs to provide nourishment for the journey to the spirit world or to symbolize the sort of funeral meal to be seen on Julia Velva's tombstone.

As far as archaeologists are concerned, one of the most valuable aspects of ancient cemeteries is that they give an insight into what the people themselves were like. Examination of the human remains allows experts to determine an individual's sex and approximate age at death. Certain types of wound, notably limb fractures, and also diseases and congenital disorders may be revealed, although it is rarely possible to identify the cause of death. To get a reliable picture of a population's physical attributes, however, it is necessary to examine a large number of bodies and this why Trentholme Drive is so important. One of the more striking features of the skeletons is that of those whose sex could be identified, there were four times as many men as women. This is surprising as ancient cemeteries usually contain an even balance of the sexes, and there is no ready explanation for the anomaly.

Infant mortality is known to have been high in Roman times (**57**), although few babies were found at Trentholme Drive. Once infancy

56 *Tombstone of Julia Brica, aged 31, and her daughter Sempronia Martina, aged 6, set up by Sempronius Martinus. Julia Brica holds an urn and her daughter a pet bird. Found in 1892 on the Mount.*

known, the latter placed at ground level so that the inscription was visible, but the expense involved would have restricted them to the rich.

Grave markers would have been necessary to preserve order in cemeteries, but again only the rich could have stood the expense of a carved stone tombstone. Another form of grave monument was the mausoleum which may in some cases have been a very elaborate structure

57 *Infant skeleton in a lead coffin from the County Hospital site north-east of the fortress (0.50 m scale).*

had been survived, life expectancy remained low in modern terms, with as much as 75 per cent of the population dying before the age of about 40. The most easily measurable physical characteristic is height and it appears that the men from Trentholme Drive were on average 1.7 m (5 ft 7 in) and women 1.55 m (5 ft 1 in). Contrary to popular myth, these figures remained more or less unchanged until the Second World War, since when there has been a slight rise, probably due to better nutrition. As in most ancient and not so ancient populations there was considerable evidence for wear and tear amongst the Trentholme Drive skeletons and arthritis was common in the over thirties. It is not usually possible to determine ethnic origins from skeletons, but one skull from the site, unfortunately dissociated from its body, was thought to have negroid features.

The civilian settlements at York – success or failure?

The theme of change in the post-Severan period will occupy the next chapter, but at this point it is useful to sum up the evidence for the civilian settlements at York at the time of the emperor's death. The excavation programme of the last 20 years or so has in my view confirmed

that by 211 the principal civilian settlement on the south-west bank of the Ouse had grown rapidly over a relatively short period of time and by the standards of Roman Britain it exhibited a fair degree of prosperity. This was probably based both on servicing the needs of the army and on a role as a regional market centre to which agricultural products were sent in large quantities, and from which manufactured goods were despatched, along with goods such as pottery, glassware and wine landed at the port of York. In short it would not be overstating the case to say that York was one of the boom towns of late second-century Britain.

On both sides of the Ouse there were clearly buildings of some size and architectural pretension, and some of the amenities of a classical city, if modest in scale by Mediterranean standards. The population was varied in its occupations and included craftsmen and merchants as well as retired legionaries and people connected with the Roman administration. We also know that, although the people may have been largely native, many of their number were drawn from other parts of the empire. Among the leading members of the community, moreover, there was the wealth to indulge in sophisticated Romanized tastes, whether in food or tombstones. All things considered, we may presume that York had a cosmopolitan atmosphere quite different from that of the nearby *civitas* capital at Aldborough or indeed of any other Roman town in Britain except the provincial capital at London.

It should also be recognized, however, that the impetus behind the development of the civilian settlements at York probably came as much from the provincial government as from private wealth. While a temporary boost to the local economy doubtless ensued from the visit of the emperor and his retinue, Caracalla's creation of York as a provincial capital with its attendant official sponsorship of, perhaps, the construction of defences and a governor's palace, would have been a vital underpinning of further growth. It must be remembered, moreover, that the *colonia* was comparatively small: the area within the medieval walls on the south-west bank of the Ouse is only *c.* 27 ha (67 acres). By comparison, the walled area of Roman London was 140 ha (346 acres) and of Trier *c.* 200 ha (500 acres). Even if the civilian areas on the north-east bank are added, the Roman town at York clearly never achieved the size or population of towns founded in the late first century in southern England, let alone of the great and many not so great urban settlements of Gaul or Germany. It would be surprising if Roman York ever had more than 3000 civilian inhabitants, while London may have come close to 10,000 at its height and Trier twice that number. York is, however, interesting because of the contrast between its proud status and modest achievements when seen from an empire-wide rather than a purely northern British point of view. The *Colonia Eboracensis*, the last major town to be founded in Roman Britain, is a very striking witness to the decreasing momentum of an economic system in which towns played a significant role.

Late Roman York

The altar dedicated at Bordeaux to the local deity, the Tutela Boudiga, by Marcus Aurelius Lunaris in 237 (see **31**) is the latest datable Roman inscription to refer to York, and few, if any, of the undated inscriptions from the city itself can be confidently considered later. The lack of late Roman inscriptions in York and their scarcity country-wide is, however, just one indication of changes in cultural attitudes and economic circumstances in the middle years of the third century throughout the western empire. A further hint of change may be contained in what presumably was the occasion of Lunaris' dedication. As a block of millstone grit it had clearly been brought from York and probably commemorated a successful sea voyage, but this acquires a particular significance when we hear from contemporary sources that a serious problem faced by sea-farers in the mid-third century was piracy, perpetrated, for the most part, by barbarians from outside the empire. Even more dangerous was the threat of full-scale incursions into imperial territory, and in 233 and 258, for example, serious attacks on Gaul and northern Italy were made by a Germanic people known as the Alamanni. As far as Britain was concerned, the principal danger was from sea-borne raids and to combat them a system of forts, known as the Saxon Shore forts, was gradually created on the south and east coasts during the third century.

One reason for the increasing insecurity of the empire and weakening of the frontier defences was that the death of the Emperor Severus Alexander in 235 was followed by a long period of internal uncertainty as rival claimants vied for the crown, each backed by sections of the army. Out of the chaos resulting

from the collapse of the Rhineland frontier there emerged in 260 a breakaway 'Empire of the Gallic Provinces' which encompassed most of Spain, Gaul and Germany as well as Britain. It was initially ruled by the army commander Postumus who succeeded in restoring the west's defences, but after his murder in 269 the Gallic Empire fell into the hands of less competent men and in 274 it collapsed leaving the Emperor Aurelian to restore unified rule from the centre.

It is not easy to determine how these political developments affected Roman Britain, one reason being the lack of good archaeological dating material for the period c.225–75. The manufacture of samian had come to an end in the early third century and the supply of coinage to Britain became intermittent, almost drying up at times. Without samian and coins it has proved difficult to recognize distinctive mid-third-century pottery groups. To some extent this may also be due to refuse disposal patterns, in the sense that buildings were kept scrupulously clean and refuse, including broken pottery, was taken away from the buildings and dumped elsewhere. The apparent lack of deposits and structures which are undeniably mid-third century may, therefore, indicate either that Roman sites were flourishing and subject to a strict cleanliness regime, or neglected – the absence of refuse being due to an absence of people. As far as York is concerned, neither option can be confidently chosen. Pottery characteristic of the mid-third century can now be identified as a result of recent research, but it has not as yet been found in anything like the same quantity as pottery of the late second or early third centuries.

In spite of the problems of dating, it may be suggested that Britain avoided the worst of the turmoil afflicting the western empire and suffered no major invasions either by way of the coast or the northern land frontier. At the same time, however, the effects of inflation and the disruption of interprovincial trade attendant on political instability probably led to significant changes in the way the economy operated. These changes may have been particularly severe in towns, which explains the virtual absence of evidence for urban growth in the mid-third century. An important aspect of the decline of towns was probably the emigration of the native aristocrats to their country estates as the opportunities for wealth through trade began to dry up and civic duties became increasingly onerous. This may account for the contrast between stagnation in towns and signs of increasing wealth on landed estates in the third and early fourth centuries, a period which may be considered the golden age of the Romano-British villa.

The fortress defences: reconstruction completed

As a result of a relatively peaceful situation in mid-third-century Britain, the army may have been run down as troops were pressed into service elsewhere. One consequence of this was that the forts and fortresses were no longer properly maintained. In the last years of the third century and early years of the fourth, however, there are signs of refurbishment and reconstruction on many military sites and it seems likely that completion of the fortress defences in stone at York formed part of this programme.

The best-known features of the work are the wall and towers on the north-west and south-west sides of the fortress, but contemporary walling is also known on the north-east side, north-west of the *porta decumana*, and on the south-east side south-west of the *porta principalis sinistra*. The greatest architectural ambition was exercised on the south-west side which incorporated a polygonal tower at the west and south corners – the former still visible as the Multangular Tower (**colour plate 9**) – and six projecting interval towers. All but one of these – SW4 – has been seen in recent years, although only the remains of SW6 are visible today. In plan the corner towers had a complex design based on a fourteen-sided figure; a circle through the internal angles would be tangential to the curve of the inner face of the fortress

wall. Four of the fourteen faces were omitted at the rear of the towers to create the entrance to a substantial structure, rectangular in plan. The projecting front parts of the interval towers were designed as half of a twelve-sided figure (**58–59**, and **colour plate 10**). The date of the recorded remains of the *porta praetoria* is unknown, but the north-west gatehouse was clearly rectangular and there is no evidence that it had a projecting front to match the towers.

The projecting towers, a feature also of the Saxon Shore forts, are a graphic indication of changing ideas on military strategy and fortification. In contrast to earlier times, when it fought in the field, the later Roman army expected to defend forts and fortresses in a manner which foreshadows the castle sieges of medieval warfare. The towers enabled the defenders to fire along the line of the walls at hostile forces attempting to scale or mine them.

While these towers were in keeping with the army's new emphasis on a defensive posture, it should at the same time be recognized that it is unlikely that the fortress at York was ever besieged. The fact that the projecting towers were confined to the south-west side of the fortress may have reflected the army's opinion that the river was the most likely avenue of attack, but the towers were probably designed as much to impress local residents and visitors as to have a military function and are a most appropriate testimony to York's role as *colonia* and provincial capital.

The wall itself was founded either on mortared rubble or substantial concrete footings set, in places, on timber piles c.0.75 m (2 ft 6 in) long. The upstanding masonry was, like the wall in the east quadrant and at Parliament Street near the south corner, c.1.5 m (5 ft/5 pM) thick at the base.

A mortared rubble core was faced on the exterior with regular courses of small limestone blocks. These were interrupted at a height of c.2.3 m (7 ft 6 in) by a band of five courses of tiles (although practice varies somewhat). There was no distinct plinth at the base of the wall, as there was in the earlier work, although the lowest course of facing stones was usually made of larger blocks than those above. Part of the cornice at the top of the wall survives in one place north-east of the Multangular Tower and was composed of tiles stepped out from the wall face. The height of the wall to

58 *Interval Tower SW5 as excavated in 1974 (2 m scale).*

the top of the cornice was *c.*5 m (16 ft 6 in). Above this there would have been a parapet, of which no trace now survives. The rear of the wall, which would have been hidden by the rampart, was only roughly finished.

It appears that the south-western defences were planned in accordance with principles employed elsewhere in the fortress, with the *pes Monetalis* as the basic unit of measurement. In addition, it is striking that once again the predeliction for a 35 pM (10.36 m/34 ft) unit is noticeable. As mentioned in Chapter 2 the distance north-west/south-east across the fortress prior to the construction of a wall was 1400 pM (1360 pM of internal space and 40 pM of rampart). When the wall was added this rose to 1405 pM (415.88 m/1364 ft) and it appears that

for the purposes of spacing the towers on the south-west front the distance was divided into nine units, eight of 160 pM (47.36 m/155 ft) and a ninth, in the centre, of 125 pM (37 m/121 ft). The end units were then modified to take the projecting corner towers. Their overall length was probably intended to be 85 pM (25.16 m/82 ft 6 in), but they also measured 70 pM (20.72 m/68 ft) from the rear of the tower to where a 90 degree corner to the fortress would have lain. The front of the tower projected 15 pM (4.44 m/14 ft 6 in) beyond this point. The diameter of the circle joining the internal

59 *(Above) The plan of Interval Tower SW5 as excavated.*

60 *(Below) The proposed metrology of the layout of Interval Tower SW5.*

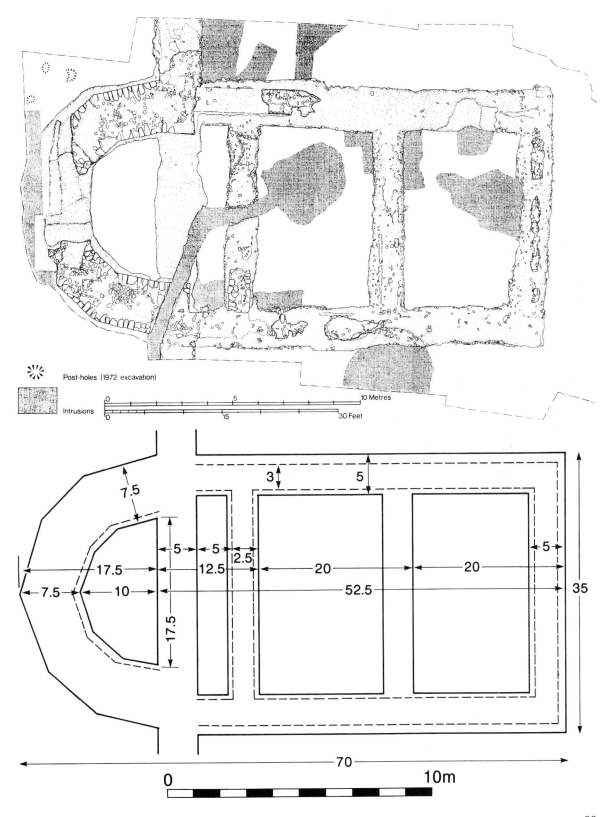

Post-holes (1972 excavation)

Intrusions

angles was probably designed to be 35 pM (10.36 m/34 ft) and the corresponding external diameter at the tower base to be 50 pM (14.8 m/48 ft 6 in).

Each of the six units of wall measuring 160 pM contained a stretch of wall 125 pM long and an interval tower which was probably intended to be 35 pM wide and 70 pM long (**60**). The towers projected 17.5 pM (5.2 m/17 ft) beyond the wall line which brought them to within 2.5 pM (0.74 m/2 ft 6 in) of the inner edge of the realigned fortress ditch (see p.58). The original height of the interval and corner towers is, of course, not known, but 35 pM (10.36 m/34 ft) would answer the requirements of symmetry.

On the north-west side of the fortress the wall was accompanied by a series of more modest interval towers. It is likely that seven existed originally, but only four have been recorded. The most recently discovered is NW1, found in 1971, and it is the only one of which remains can be seen today. The locations of NW4, and NW6 and NW7 can be conjectured on the basis of some form of regular spacing. All the towers known were rectangular in plan and lay behind the line of the wall, but probably projected the same distance above it as those on the south-west front. The tower sides measure *c*.6 m (20 ft) which was probably intended to be 20 pM. The plan of the south-west gatehouse of the north-west gate (*porta principalis dextra*) is known and a recent observation at Bootham Bar appeared to show that it was contemporary with the curtain wall. It is not known if an earlier stone gateway stood here.

In the absence of sufficient information, the metrology of the wall and towers on the north-west defences is not easy to work out with confidence. The discovery of tower NW1 suggests, however, that the spacing of the towers between the west corner and the *porta principalis dextra* was also based on units of 160 pM (47.36 m/155 ft).

As far as the rampart is concerned, it appears that, at the time of the wall and towers described above, there was reconstruction along the lines of the work in the east quadrant as described in Chapter 3 (pp.58–9). At Interval Tower NW5 Miller found *c*.5 m (16 ft 6 in) of rampart behind the tower which suggests an overall width of *c*.11 m (36 ft). South-west of the Anglian Tower the 1971 excavations found the rampart standing some 4 m (13 ft)

above ground level, rather higher than at the east corner.

Artefactual material for dating the wall, towers, rampart and ditches described above is extremely sparse. The usually accepted late third- or early fourth-century date is based primarily on just two coins. One of them is of Claudius Gothicus (268–70) and came from 8 Coney Street in a layer thought to be in the refurbished rampart. The other coin, of Tetricus I (271–3), was found by Miller in the rampart at Interval Tower NW5 along with a sherd of a *mortarium* (mixing-bowl) of late third-century type. Finally we may note the evidence of the ditch on the south-west side. At Interval Towers SW5 and SW6 the ditch appears to have been deliberately realigned to accommodate the towers; confirmation of this may be found in Miller's discovery that it curved outwards slightly to go around the Multangular Tower. The realigned ditch and towers can, in short, be presumed contemporary. Pottery from the Interval Tower SW5 site has been examined in the light of the latest research and suggests that the earliest ditch cut on the new line had probably begun to fill up by the end of the third century when a recut was made.

In the absence of conclusive artefactual material for dating the structures under discussion, consideration must also be given to stylistic affinities. While the distinctive projecting towers have parallels in military and civilian fortifications of the later third or early fourth century, there are also earlier parallels. Projecting seven-sided polygonal towers are, for example, known from the south gate of the fort at Risingham, north of Hadrian's Wall, which can be dated by an inscription to as early as 205–8. As the third century wore on projecting towers, of semicircular and rectangular as well as polygonal form, became more common, occurring in Britain at the Saxon Shore forts such as Burgh Castle and Richborough and at the fort at Cardiff.

In view of the likely late third-century date for the completion of the defences in stone, a few further comments may be made on the design of the work described above. First of all, the small internal towers on the north-west side of the fortress are virtually unknown elsewhere in contemporary contexts and should probably be explained as deliberately archaic and intended to match earlier towers such as NE6. Secondly, the metrological evidence appears to show that the design, particularly on the south-west side, was conceived in accordance with principles found in construction work datable to the late first and mid-second centuries. There is, for example, a continued use of the distinctive 35 pM unit which links the towers with late first- and second-century planning episodes in the fortress. An implication of this may be that the structures were laid out by application of Roman surveying principles introduced to York by the *agrimensores* of the ninth legion in 71 and handed down to their successors some 200 years later.

York – a late Roman capital

The material evidence for Roman Britain in general and Roman York in particular in the later third and first half of the fourth centuries is, like that for the early third century, relatively plentiful. Coinage from the later years of the Gallic Empire is abundant and became so again in the reign of Constantine I and his sons (307–61). As far as pottery is concerned, the last quarter of the third century was a time when a number of important late Roman industries began production. In York the distinctive wares of the kilns at Crambeck, southwest of Malton, appear in large quantities in later Roman deposits.

A revival in the fortunes of the western empire in the late third century was to a large extent due to a reassertion of governmental control at the centre which began during the rule of the Emperior Diocletian (284–305). Running the empire at the best of times was an extremely taxing job for one man and so Diocletian established a system called the Tetrarchy, both to lessen the burden and provide for a more ordered succession. There were now four emperors, one senior (the Augustus) and one junior (the Caesar), for both the eastern and western halves of the empire. Diocletian also subdivided the provinces again. Where Britain had been two as a result of Caracalla's reform, it now became four and a new tier of administration, the Diocese, was established. This was administered by an official known as the Vicar of Britain with his capital at London (now known as Augusta) who was, in turn, answerable to the Prefect of the Gauls in Trier. York remained a capital, but of a slightly smaller province than before, known as *Britannia Secunda*. In addition, at about the same time, the military and civilian spheres were separated so that the provincial governors were no longer in charge of troops. The new system was more bureaucratic than the old, but served to keep the western empire together for another 100 years or so.

In a political sense Britain's situation in the late third century was complicated by a further secessionist episode as a result of the revolt in 285 of Carausius, a Roman naval commander. In 293 he was murdered and his successor Allectus was defeated by Constantius I, then the Caesar in the west, in 296. Some ten years later, while campaigning in the north, Constantius, by now the Augustus in the west, was to become the second emperor to die in York. On his death the Tetrarchy system demanded that the Caesar in the west, one Flavius Valerius Severus, should be promoted Augustus, but, urged on by a king of the Alamanni named Crocus who was serving with the Roman army in Britain, Constantius' troops voted for his son Constantine. Over the next eighteen years Constantine gradually finished off his rivals and in 324 emerged as supreme ruler of the empire.

Constantine I, 'the Great', is, perhaps, best known for his acceptance of Christianity and for making it an official religion of the Roman state. At the same time, paradoxical though it may seem, Constantine's reign saw worship of the emperor as a superhuman, if not divine, being reach new heights. We can get some flavour of this from the panegyrics which were offered to the emperor on state occasions. One example composed by the poet Eumenius also shows how Britain, as a place where Constantine came to power, was able to bask in some reflected glory. 'Fortunate and happier than all lands, because she first saw Constantine Caesar' he wrote and then goes on:

> Gracious gods! What means this, that always from some remote end of the world, new deities descend to be universally revered? Truly places nearer to heaven are more sacred than inland regions; and it was very proper that an Emperor should be sent by the gods, from the region [i.e. Britain] in which the earth terminates.

Another expression of the emperor's quasi-divine status which became popular in the fourth century was the larger than life monumental statue. As a bust taken to be his likeness was found in Stonegate in the early

101

nineteenth century we may imagine that an example depicting Constantine stood before the headquarters at York (**colour plate 11**). This may, however, have been just one part of a general refurbishment of the headquarters building itself in Constantine's reign. Excavations at the Minster showed that the basilica was reorganized internally with, for example, the addition of a room at the north-west end which filled in the portico space and was decorated with very fine painted wall plaster (**colour plate 7**).

The occasion of the changes to the basilica may have been the installation at York of an official known as the *Dux Britanniarum* who is referred to in the *Notitia Dignitatum*, a list of official and military dispositions, probably dating to the early fifth century, but incorporating earlier material. It is clear from the *Notitia Dignitatum* and other sources that the organization of the Roman army in the fourth century had changed considerably since the early days of conquest. The first-century army had relied primarily on the legions attached to particular provinces and based on or near the frontiers. It was assumed that the empire would continue to expand and the legions would continue to move into forward positions. By the time of Constantine, however, the empire had long since ceased to expand and the army had adopted a defence in depth approach geared primarily to repelling invaders and making the frontiers secure. It was now found more useful to have a mobile field force, largely mounted, which could be moved to trouble spots as required. The frontiers themselves came to be manned by troops known as *limitanei* who may be thought of as a local militia raised from the native population. Some indication of the new arrangements has come down to us through the *Notitia Dignitatum*, which suggests that military commanders now had responsibility for areas rather than specific bodies of men, although it also indicates that York remained the base of a unit known as the sixth legion. The *Dux Britanniarum* was, however, probably in charge of all troops in the north of Britain, both detachments of the field army and the frontier guards.

In spite of the continuing military importance of the York fortress, little evidence has yet been found for construction work in the early fourth century, except at the headquarters building and at a site in Low Petergate where part of a new stone building was found. All that can be added to this is a remetalling of the *intervallum* at Bedern Trench 3/4 after the accumulation of a layer of silt on the late second-century surface and the redigging of the fortress ditch at Interval Towers SW5 and SW6.

The civilian settlements

As far as the civilian settlements at York are concerned, their fate in the mid-third century remains obscure, but new construction work was set in train in the later third and early fourth centuries. There is no better place to begin a survey of the evidence than the Queen's Hotel site where the early third-century building referred to above (pp. 87–8) was replaced towards the end of the century (**61–62**). Two major walls were examined in detail, each of which was *c*.2.2 m (7 ft) thick. Together with others not fully excavated, they survived to a height of up to 3.5 m (11 ft 6 in), although *c*.1.5 m (5 ft) had been below-ground footing. The stone used was oolitic limestone, but the construction technique of employing intermediate tile courses recalls the fortress wall described above. Both of the fully excavated walls also had brick-lined arches in them. The building floors were originally made of *opus signinum*. Subsequent developments, probably in the early fourth century, may have included the addition of rooms to the south-east.

The function of the structure of which these walls form part is, like that of its predecessor, unknown, although the presence of a large drain set into the principal wall examined might suggest a bath house and the architectural style is reminiscent of so-called 'Constantinian' baths at Arles and Trier. Whatever the remains at Queen's Hotel were part of, it is of the greatest interest for understanding the status of late Roman York that a major public building was constructed in the *colonia* in the late third century, a period in which it is difficult to find anything comparable taking place in the other Roman towns of Britain.

Elsewhere in the *colonia* there is evidence for the construction of substantial late Roman residences. Fine fourth-century mosaics found in the nineteenth century suggest the presence of two examples in the north-western quarter. The mosaics themselves are taken to be products of a local school of mosaicists whose work is also known in Aldborough and in

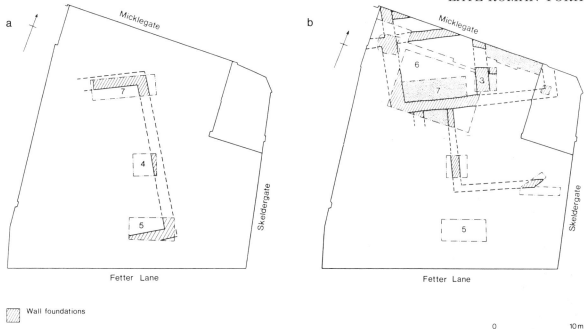

a

Micklegate

7

4

5

Skeldergate

Fetter Lane

b

Micklegate

6

3

7

5

Skeldergate

Fetter Lane

▨ Wall foundations

╌╌╌ Conjectured line of walls

▢ Evidence for opus signinum floors

0   10 m

0   30 ft

61 *(Above) Plans showing the walls excavated at the Queen's Hotel (1–9 Micklegate) site: a early third century; b late third/early fourth-century.*

62 *(Below) Wall of a late third-century public building at the Queen's Hotel (1–9 Micklegate) site, looking south-west (2 m scale). A brick-lined arch, blocked in the fourth century, can be clearly seen.*

63 *The apse of a late Roman town house at St Mary Bishophill Junior excavated by Peter Wenham in 1964 (3ft scale).*

villas around Brough-on-Humber. One of the pavements, found along with two others on Toft Green in 1853, has a design incorporating, at the corners, female busts representing the four seasons (**colour plate 12**). Spring is symbolized by a bird, summer by a rake, autumn by a bunch of grapes and winter by a bare bough. The seasons are a common theme on British mosaics as befits a country which was overwhelmingly agricultural, but of additional interest in this mosaic is the depiction of a bust of the gorgon Medusa in the centre. In Greek legend Medusa's ghastly face turned all who gazed upon it to stone. In many Roman representations, as at York on the Toft Green mosaic and the jet medallions (see **49**), the face was made conventionally female with only the odd wild locks of hair. Nevertheless, it would have been thought to attract and hold the powers of evil.

Part of another town house was found immediately north-west of the medieval church of St Mary Bishophill Junior. Although the walls had been heavily robbed, the building had probably been quite extensive with at least two ranges of rooms around a courtyard. An apse (**63**) had been added to one wing during the life of the building, essentially as an architectural flourish to enhance its appearance, and it may have been used as the focus for a large *triclinium*. At St Mary Bishophill Senior

64 *Remains of a large house at Clementhorpe. The walls have been heavily robbed, but it is possible to identify the apsed* triclinium *in the centre and a room upper left which has a mosaic pavement (2m scale). The bath-shaped pits are graves of medieval St Clement's nunnery.*

there is again an apse forming part of the upgrading of a modest earlier stone house which probably consisted of several wings around a courtyard. In the wing most extensively examined there were four rooms connected by a corridor, and three of them had under-floor heating supplied by a furnace attached to the outside wall.

Equally important evidence for prosperous town houses has been found outside the walled town south-west of the Ouse. At the Clementhorpe site (see **1**, **6**), a little to the south-east and close to the river, a large house had been erected in the early fourth century, of which three rooms were excavated in 1976–7 (**64**). The

65 *Early fourth-century mosaic at Clementhorpe.*

principal room had an apse added to it, again as a secondary feature. Rather than being semicircular, however, it was polygonal in form recalling, and perhaps this was deliberate, the towers on the south-west front of the fortress. Among the room's other appointments were painted, plastered walls and a floor of red tesserae (small rectangular tiles). In an adjacent room, were the remains of a mosaic. Only the border survived, but there was sufficient to establish a date, on stylistic grounds, of 325–50. Testimony to the use of braziers to heat the room was found in scorch marks on the mosaic's surface.

On the north-east bank of the Ouse the discovery of a mosaic was recorded at the church of St Mary Castlegate in 1871, but there are no details. In 1972 another mosaic, dated to the early fourth century, was found in excavations on the Ebor Brewery site (see **1**, **2**) near the east corner of the fortress. As at Clementhorpe it was much battered, but clearly featured a woman's bust in a round panel set centrally in a square area with a lozenge pattern. The floor had been subjected to much wear and had been patched in places with coal and samian sherds. Because of the intrusion of the medieval church of St Helen, little trace of the building which the mosaic had adorned survived, but presumably it had been another sizeable town house.

Although the evidence is admittedly patchy, there is enough to show that the civilian settlements of early fourth-century York contained a number of fine houses. In view of, on the one hand, sparse evidence for manufacturing and long distance trade at this time, but, on the other, the good evidence for the continuing importance of York as a military and administrative centre, it is possible that these houses were occupied by government officials and retired soldiers and their families rather than by merchants or wealthy artisans. The development of urban dwellings in York in the later third and fourth centuries should also be seen alongside the continuing growth of country villas in the region which may now have become the principal residences of such wealthy native Britons as were formerly based in York.

Villas around York

In a British context a villa may best be defined as a Romanized house in a rural setting which usually had a farm attached to it. The house would be built largely of stone and enjoy such appointments as heated rooms, baths and mosaic floors. In the south of England villas had existed since the late first century, their farms prospering as a result of new markets for agricultural products to which access was facilitated by the improvement of road and water communications. Villa development appears to have been much slower in the north of England and was principally a third- and fourth-century phenomenon. There is, however, nothing to compare with the great villas in the south and west of England which may, up to a point, indicate that the north was less productive agriculturally, but also, perhaps, that people here were rather less ready to absorb the Romanized cultural values which villas epitomize.

There is no evidence at present that York was, like some of the towns of Britain, a focus for villa sites. This may to some extent be because of the existence of a legionary *territorium*. Civilian landowners in the area may, moreover, have been veterans and government officials who, unlike the native aristocrats, preferred to have their principal dwelling in a town.

The nearest villa to York, and one of the few in the north of England to be extensively explored, was at Dalton Parlours. It is *c*.18 km (11 miles) south-west of York and 4 km (2½ miles) south of Wetherby, on the magnesian limestone belt. The origins of the site lie in the late pre-Roman Iron Age, but the villa was probably established in the third century and the principal buildings were erected in the early fourth. In addition to Dalton Parlours

there are a number of other possible villas on the west side of York, but it may be significant that the two which appear to be most extensive are also on the well-drained fertile soils of the magnesian limestone belt at Castle Dykes and Well near Ripon. Part of a mosaic from the latter can still be seen in Well church.

There are also a number of villas to the north-east and east of York which may have been closely linked to the small town at Malton (*Derventio*). The sites include Beadlam near Helmsley where there is the only villa building to be seen today north of the Humber. This is a small house which had heated rooms and a mosaic floor and it lay on the north side of a courtyard surrounded by other buildings, only one of which has been excavated. Further east there are villas in favourable spots in the Wolds which include Rudston and Langton where modest farms developed into larger villas in the fourth century. In the residential block and bath suite at Rudston were mosaics which are justly famous for their representations of Venus and Mercury. They bear witness to an interest in classical mythology even in this remote corner of the Roman world.

Christianity

The mosaics in these villas and in York itself show that both prosperous town dwellers and members of the landed gentry retained a consuming interest in religious matters. In the early fourth century a prominent topic of discussion was doubtless the merits of Christianity, the new faith which was spreading rapidly into the western empire. Christianity has many similarities with the 'mystery' cults in having a theology which offered believers personal salvation and everlasting life. Christianity also, of course, offered the idea of the brotherhood of man, and the injunction to love one's neighbour gave it the unique and universal appeal to all sections of the community, rich and poor, men and women, Roman and barbarian, which other cults lacked. At the same time, Christians suffered from persecution because they would not accept the existence of other gods, including the divine emperor. In due course Christianity proved strong enough to survive and it may have been a recognition of this, rather than his legendary vision before the battle at the Milvian bridge in 312, which persuaded Constantine to accept the faith and turn its strength to his advantage.

Evidence for Christianity in Roman Britain comes largely from towns and villas, which may indicate that it was principally a religion of the upper echelons of society who travelled and came in contact with foreign influences, rather than one taken up by the rural masses who remained true to their native deities. There may also have been a regional aspect to the spread of Christianity since the bulk of the buildings and artefacts which can be associated with the faith have come from south of the Humber and there is as yet little evidence from the north. We know, however, that there must have been a Christian community in Roman York since a bishop existed by 314 when 'Eborius, the bishop for the city of York' was summoned by Constantine with three others from Britain to the Council of Arles to discuss doctrinal matters. Archaeological traces of Christianity in York are confined to just two artefacts. There is a tile from the Minster excavations bearing the chi-rho monogram (☧), the first two letters of Christ's name in Greek, and a bone plaque bearing a motto thought to be in Christian style: S(O)ROR AVE VIVAS IN DEO (O sister, hail! May you have life in God) was found with a burial in a stone coffin (**colour plate 13**).

It has been suggested that evidence for the spread of Christianity in Roman Britain can be elicited from burial customs. The emphasis on spiritual over material values which would preclude grave goods may, the argument goes, explain the large number of late Roman unfurnished graves. In addition, the fact that the bodies were usually laid out with their heads at the west end of the grave would allow them to rise and face east at the sound of the 'Last Trump' from the Holy Land. Unfortunately, the relationship between burial customs and religion is a complex one. East–west burial could be related to religious beliefs, but it may also indicate a purely practical concern to use the position of the sunrise to organize a cemetery in an orderly fashion. As regards the question of grave furnishing, the fact that the bone plaque with the Christian motto was found in a burial with a glass jug and other objects shows that one cannot regard the presence of furnishing as an indication of a non-Christian interment or vice versa.

The belief in resurrection on the Day of Judgement has also prompted an association with Christianity of the distinctive late Roman practice of embalming the body of the deceased in gypsum (calcium sulphate), usually within a stone or lead coffin. There are some 50 gypsum burials known from York, of which 17 are thought to be of certain fourth-century date. Their find spots are not distributed such as to suggest a distinct area for Christian burial, however, and it is probably correct to conclude that gypsum burial was simply a fashionable and expensive form of late Roman interment with no obvious religious connotations.

While explicit evidence for Christianity is difficult to identify in late Roman burials, there are signs in the cemeteries of fourth-century York of a change in attitudes to the sanctity of earlier graves. At 35–41 Blossom Street the third-century cemetery described in the previous chapter had fallen into disuse by the early fourth century when the mausoleum was deliberately dismantled. Subsequently, a fourth-century cemetery was established which contained some 25 graves aligned north-west/south-east, at 90 degrees to the earlier interments. A number of graves also cut into the remains of the mausoleum and burials within it. The fourth-century burials were in wooden coffins, but unfurnished except for those of infants (**66**). A break with previous traditions, involving abrupt changes in burial orientation and furnishing practice, can be paralleled in other Romano-British cemeteries in the early fourth century and could indicate the spread of Christianity, but this cannot be proved at present.

There is also evidence from elsewhere for the destruction of temples and funerary monuments which could have been the work of Christians. This may be the context not only for the demolition of the mausoleum at Blossom Street, but also for the disturbance of other prominent burials of earlier times at York. The sarcophagus of Aelia Severa, for example, did not contain the body of the lady herself, but that of an adult male, and the tombstone of a woman named Flavia Augustina had been reused as a lid. The sarcophagi of Julia Fortunata and of a Julia Victorina also contained adult male skeletons.

Roman York – the last rites

The reigns of Constantine and his sons were an era of strong government for the Roman Empire and for a while invaders were successfully repelled and the economy revived. More

66 *A fourth-century infant burial with shale bracelets from the 35–41 Blossom Street cemetery.*

troubled times returned to the west after the usurpation of Magnentius (350–3), another in a long line of army commanders who had ideas above their station. After defeating Magnentius, Constantius II (337–61) restored unified rule, but imperial security in the west suffered one disastrous blow after another in the second half of the fourth century. One of these, the so-called 'Barbarian Conspiracy' of 367, was recorded by the contemporary historian Ammianus Marcellinus. By some unlucky chance, a number of barbarian forces from Scotland and Ireland and from across the North Sea attacked Britain at the same time. They found the Roman army unequal to repelling them, a senior Roman officer was killed and the *Dux*, one Fullofaudes, put out of action.

In the aftermath of the events of 367 Ammianus reported that the Emperor Valentinian

sent a high-ranking official, Count Theodosius, to restore Britain's defences. Identifying building work which can be securely dated to the late 360s is impossible but as far as York is concerned, a fortification which may belong to the later fourth century is the so-called 'Anglian Tower' (**67**). This is a rectangular stone structure about 60 m (200 ft) north-east of the Multangular Tower, which was originally discovered in 1842 and re-excavated in 1970. The tower now stands *c*.4 m (13 ft) high and measures *c*.4.5 m (14 ft 6 in) square. It is built of roughly coursed and dressed oolitic limestone in contrast to the vast majority of the fortress buildings which are of magnesian limestone. There are opposing doorways with simple arches; the original roof was replaced with a brick barrel vault in the nineteenth century. The tower wall footings are shallow, but the front of the structure was founded on the base of a cut into the fortress wall.

The 1970 excavation was not able to offer any conclusive evidence on the date of the tower, although it was shown to be later than the fortress wall and earlier than a stone

67 *The 'Anglian' tower, probably late fourth century, set into the late third-century fortress wall. The Multangular Tower is at the top right.*

revetted bank which sat on top of the Roman rampart. This bank was considered to have been a replacement of the wall's derelict parapet and contained one or two sherds of Anglian pottery. One reason for suggesting a post-Roman date for the tower appears to be the notion that the cut into the fortress wall was an enhancement of a gap already created by dilapidation. This must have taken place, so the argument continues, after the Roman army had departed since it would surely have repaired the wall had it been in residence. The fortress wall is, however, a very strong structure and unlikely to be prone to much deterioration even over two to three hundred years. Even if this had happened, there is no reason for a tower rather than a stretch of walling to be used to plug a gap. It might equally well be asked, of course, why a tower was needed in Roman times since there was already a perfectly good one, NW1, nearby. The answer may be that Interval Tower NW1 had become unsafe. In the 1971 excavation to expose the fortress wall the tower walls were found to have parted from it, probably due to subsidence, the effects of which have been observed in several other places around the fortress wall circuit. If NW1 had subsided in the Roman period this would provide a simple explanation for a fourth-century replacement nearby.

Another argument for giving the Anglian Tower a late Roman date has been developed by Dr Paul Buckland of Sheffield University and rests on his analysis of the building stone. Jurassic oolite was, as already noted, extensively used in Roman York, but there is no evidence for its further use until medieval times. No newly-built Anglian stone buildings are known in the city and the stone used in the Anglo-Scandinavian period, particularly for churches, was largely if not exclusively salvaged from redundant Roman buildings. The fact that the Anglian Tower contains no reused stone implies, Buckland suggests, that the Roman fortress buildings were still in use and therefore, he concludes, the tower must be Roman.

A further addition to the north's late Roman defences was a series of signal stations on the Yorkshire coast between Filey and Huntcliff (see 4). The invaders of 367 may have come around Hadrian's Wall by boat to the unprotected coastline and the signal stations were intended to prevent a recurrence of this. They were essentially towers defended by a bank and ditch – 'turrum et castrum' as described on an inscription from the station at Ravenscar. The height of the towers is unknown, but as much as 30 m (100 ft) is possible. At the top there was presumably a signalling beacon which could be used to co-ordinate Roman naval patrols and contact the fort at Malton where a unit known as the *Numerus Supervenientium Petuariensium* – 'the anticipators of Petuaria [Brough-on-Humber]' – was stationed. If matters were really serious, then presumably the army at York could be called out.

The imperial authorities must have hoped that Theodosius had secured Britain for the foreseeable future, but if so they were over-optimistic. In the last two or three decades of the fourth century both archaeological and written evidence show the beginnings of radical change in the established order. One reason for this was probably a gradual diminution in the size of the Roman forces in Britain as a succession of usurpers, of whom Magnus Maximus in 383 was but the first, removed troops from York and elsewhere to challenge for the imperial crown. By c.410, the date frequently given for the end of Britain's inclusion in the Roman empire, there can have been few soldiers worthy to be considered heirs to the proud tradition of Petilius Cerialis and his men of 71.

Archaeological evidence for the last years of the Roman era in York is sparse and the subject requires a great deal of further research. In the fortress it would appear that from c.380 onwards the character of occupation in the headquarters building, the first cohort barracks, and the buildings at 9 Blake Street, changed markedly, being characterized by the rapid accumulation of deposits containing considerable quantities of refuse including animal bone and broken pottery. At 9 Blake Street (68) the principal building range had been largely demolished by the end of the fourth century, although the north-western wall still stood. The service range, however, appears to have remained in use throughout the century and layers containing coins dated after 388 were overlain by mortar floors and refuse deposits. The street on the south-west side of the site and the passage between the buildings were resurfaced from time to time. It is not entirely clear what is signified by the changes in layout and standards of maintenance revealed here, although they

68 *9 Blake Street: late fourth-century features cut by medieval intrusions (looking north-east). Beyond the rear wall of the barracks (foreground) a 2 m-scale rests on loam deposits covering the latest surface of a cobbled street. Behind lies the service range of the buildings with a series of stone 'bases' immediately to the left of the dividing wall. At the top of the picture beyond the passage way (with a second 2 m-scale resting on it), is the main room of the residential block.*

presumably indicate a collapse of the traditional military order which may, perhaps, have given way to a regime which allowed civilians to take up residence in the fortress.

To examine the later years of Roman York in the *colonia*, we must return to the Wellington Row site. Until the excavations of 1988–90, archaeological evidence for the last years of the *colonia* had been even more elusive than in the fortress. One obstacle to research was the

extent of disturbance of late Roman deposits and structures by later pits and cellars, but at Wellington Row a remarkable sequence of deposits and structural remains was preserved which can be dated to the late fourth century and probably extends into the early fifth. The site also proved the value, if proof was needed, of excavating large areas where the characteristically ephemeral remains of late Roman structures can be identified.

The latest floor surface in the stone building at Wellington Row was a very rough and ready affair of cobbles and beaten earth which probably dates to *c*.360 (**69**). It was on this surface that a dark silty loam began to accumulate containing large quantities of artefacts, mostly pottery and animal bones. Within *c*.2 m (6 ft 6 in) or so of the surviving stone roof support pillar, however, several hundred small bronze coins were found, dating largely to the mid-fourth century. It is possible that these coins were casually dropped or swept in with

69 *Wellington Row: the latest Roman surface within the stone building dated c.360–80 (2 m scale)*

refuse, but an alternative interpretation, in view of their remarkable spatial concentration, is that they were deliberately placed here perhaps as part of a hoard which was later disturbed. At the time of excavation it was my view that they must have had a votive context given the frequent use of coins as ritual offerings in the Roman world. Some support for this theory was provided by several other unusual and more or less contemporary features including the deliberate burials, close to the pillar stone, firstly of a pot (**70**) and secondly of a lamb's skeleton in a small pit. If the theory of a sacred context for these finds can be sustained, then this may be a building which, at least briefly, was used as a roadside shrine of some

sort. Whether this has any implications for its earlier history is unknown.

After *c*.380 further deposits of dark loam built up within the building to a depth of *c*.0.80 m (2 ft 6 in) in places. Comparable material, often known as 'dark earth', is a common phenomenon on urban sites in Britain overlying the latest identifiable Roman structures and pre-dating those of late Anglo-Saxon/Anglo-Scandinavian or medieval date. The forces creating the dark earth are varied, but analysis suggests that a substantial component was probably decaying plant material, dead leaves and the like, mixed with domestic and other refuse. As a result a common feature of the dark earth both in York and elsewhere is that it contains a large quantity of artefacts (**71**). This need not, however, mean that late Roman towns were densely populated. Instead it may indicate a changed approach to refuse

70 *Wellington Row – Y.A.T. Excavation Assistant Sarah-Jane Farr excavating a fourth-century pot deliberately buried close to the roof support pillar at the south-east end of the stone building.*

disposal involving a lowering of standards and a change of use for areas previously in occupation. It was obviously easier to get rid of latrine matter or domestic rubbish by throwing it into a disused building near one's home than it was to carry it some distance to an extramural dump. In dark earth deposits found in trenches across the centre of the Wellington Row site the artefacts were finely broken up suggesting a reworking of the material by agriculture, datable by a small number of pot sherds to the Anglian period. Within the stone building, however, pottery and bone occurred in large pieces and had clearly not been disturbed after deposition. The building itself probably became derelict as wind and rain eroded away the mortar between the stones in the exposed parts of the walls of what was by *c*.400 essentially a large rectangular rubbish pit. The contents

may well have been dumped by people coming along the Roman road from other parts of the *colonia*, but much of it may have been generated in buildings sited on the road surface itself in the immediate locality (**72**).

At some stage in the fourth century the great main road had been narrowed to perhaps half its width and timber structures were erected on the disused surface. Little can be said about them as the remains only survived modern cellars in a very restricted area, but a number of post bases packed around with cobbles were found along with a sequence of pebble and mortar floors. Behind the building remains, and probably contemporary in origin with them, a most remarkable trench was found. It measured *c*.2 m (6 ft 6 in) wide and 1 m (3 ft 4 in) deep and cut into the road, following its alignment. The trench sides were more or less vertical and the base was flat; cut into them was a series of slots and post-holes in which iron nails survived. These features must indicate that the trench had a wooden lining and this was probably intended to aid retention of water. The trench was, therefore, probably a simple version of the

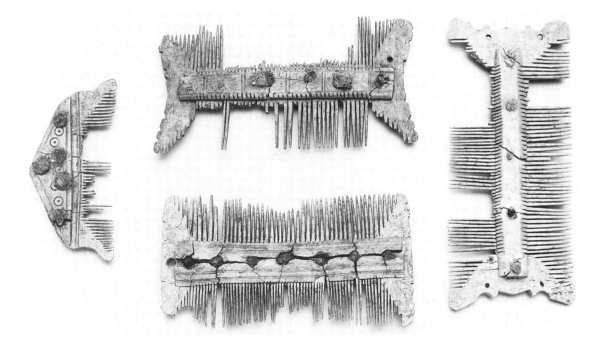

71 *A group of bone combs from the late fourth-century 'dark earth' deposits at Wellington Row.*

stone-lined channel with lead pipes which was laid down in the mid second century. Interestingly enough, there was evidence that efforts had been made to dig the earlier feature out at much the same time as wood-lined trench was installed. The content of the latter was a clean silt with none of the domestic refuse one would have expected if the filling had taken place at a time when the surrounding area was still populated to any great extent. This may indicate that the water supply to Roman York was not abandoned until the early part of the fifth century rather than in the late fourth.

The history of the road itself in the late fourth and fifth centuries could not be determined as the main carriageway now lies beyond the site, under modern Tanner Row. In the main excavation area, however, the dark earth is not the end of our story since on its surface there were traces of another building. This would have been a timber structure, but it had been erected within and reusing the remains of the original stone building. The walls may, in fact, have been deliberately taken down in places, perhaps because they had become dangerously unstable. The new building was represented, firstly, by a sill wall (**73**) on a north-east/south-

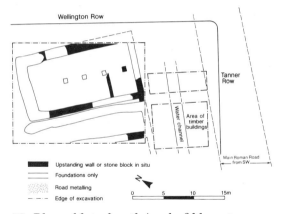

72 *Plan of late fourth-/early fifth-century features at Wellington Row.*

west line which divided off the south-eastern third of the stone building. This wall with its offset course and blocks set diagonally appears to be Roman in style, although it was poorly made and bonded with earth not mortar. To the south-east there may have been posts resting on the stone roof-support pillars which still projected above the dark earth. To the north-west of the sill wall was a rough clay surface, but whether this was internal or external is uncertain.

The date of this new structure is as yet unknown. Coins provisionally suggest it must

115

73 *Wellington Row: A stone sill wall constructed on top of the 'dark earth' deposits which may belong to a building of the late fourth/early fifth century (1 m scale).*

be after *c*.390, but any more accurate suggestion of its earliest possible date depends on an estimate of how long it took the dark earth to accumulate. The problems of dating these and other late deposits on Roman sites is that they may contain large quantities of artefacts which have been traditionally seen as Roman, mostly because they cannot be associated with any coins later than *c*.402 when the supply to Britain ceased. It is likely, however, that coins circulated for a while after 402 before finding their way into the ground. Furthermore, it seems probable that pottery in Roman style was still made in the first quarter of the fifth century, but the wares cannot as yet be positively identified. In the light of these problems it can be suggested only that the structure at Wellington Row may belong to the last years of the fourth century, but could, strictly speaking, be any date before the tenth century when

the stone walls on the site were extensively robbed.

Evidence from other sites for the end of the civilian settlements is relatively poor. At St Mary Bishophill Senior the building's hypocaust is thought to have become obsolete before the end of the fourth century, although occupation may have continued. In the house at St Mary Bishophill Junior it is apparent that there was a change in the character of occupation towards the end of the fourth century when the drains were reorganized in a rather rough and ready manner and a dump of refuse containing rotten fish was made. Late Roman refuse dumping in the form of dark earth has also been identified at other sites, including General Accident, 5 Rougier Street and 37–8 Bishophill Senior, but the deposits were heavily disturbed by medieval pits and robbing trenches.

An indication of the changes in the late Roman urban order at York as striking as the encroachment of buildings on to the main road is the intrusion of burials into previously settled areas. As elsewhere in the western empire, the sanctity of the town boundary as a division between areas devoted to the living and the dead had ceased to exercise its former power. On the south-west bank of the Ouse several late Roman inhumations in lead coffins were apparently found within the city walls during construction of the Old Station. On the north-east bank at 16–22 Coppergate the excavations encountered a small cemetery of six inhumation graves, probably of the mid to late fourth century, close to where there had been stone buildings. The bodies had been buried either north-east/south-west (4) or north-west/south-east (2) in wooden coffins placed in simple grave pits. They were unfurnished except in one case where a string of beads was found, and in another a group of iron hobnails indicated that the individual's boots had been buried with him.

The impression has sometimes been created in archaeological literature that the sort of changes in the urban order outlined above were symptomatic of a collapse into anarchy at the end of the Roman period. This should not, however, be the picture that immediately springs to mind when considering York in the late fourth and early fifth centuries. Rather, the situation should be seen in terms of a reordering of priorities at a time when an urban economy based on servicing the military and the provincial government was proving impossible to sustain. There was, of course, a decline in standards of building and road maintenance and a diminution of population, but the end of Roman York in the sense of the final disappearance of all or most of its people arrived not with a disorderly bang as the barbarians rushed in, but with a dignified whimper.

Postscript – a city reborn

Although the archaeological evidence for the fifth to sixth centuries is virtually non-existent, it cannot be assumed that what had been Roman York was either entirely deserted or lacking a role in the economy and society of the region. In a period when imperial power had probably devolved to competing local warlords the importance of York as both a defendable stronghold and crucial river crossing is unlikely to have been overlooked. It can be imagined, furthermore, that an awareness of Roman York's former role as a centre of political and religious authority continued to impose itself on the local population. For anyone tempted to revive such authority the city also, of course, possessed the appropriate, if somewhat run-down amenities for the associated functions and ceremonies. As yet evidence for any such revival is scarce, although the Minster excavations suggested a continuing occupation of the fortress headquarters building for a somewhat ill-defined period after 400.

In the first instance, control of post-Roman York may have been assumed by a British kingdom known as Elmet, which is thought to have occupied much of Yorkshire to the west of the city. Fifth- to-sixth-century settlements of the incoming Anglians north of the Humber appear to be largely confined to the former East Riding, but evidence for a pagan Anglian population in the York area in the later fifth-sixth century comes from two cremation cemeteries, one at Heworth and the other on The Mount. Both of them were sited close to main Roman roads, which, we may suppose, were still in use, and they also lay within areas of Roman cemetery suggesting, perhaps, some continuity of sacred associations. In the early seventh century we hear that Elmet was conquered by King Edwin of Northumbria. He was to return York to the mainstream of written history in 627 when, as the Venerable Bede tells us, he had himself baptized here in a small wooden church.

The survival of the Roman roads around York and streets within it may constitute some of the more telling evidence for continuing occupation in the post-Roman period, although only excavation can show if they were actively maintained. It is still apparent today, however, that Petergate, Stonegate and Chapter House Street run on the lines of the principal fortress thoroughfares (see 8). In the south-east quadrant of the fortress the line of the south-westernmost intermediate street appears to survive as the north-east side of St Sampson's Square and as Little Stonegate. A short stretch of the south-east *intervallum* survives as Church Street.

On the south-west bank of the Ouse excavations at Wellington Row were not able to determine the post-Roman fate of the main route from the south-west, but it was probably moved early in the Anglo-Scandinavian period to its present line along Micklegate. The Roman road and river crossing, if not necessarily the bridge, probably survived up to this time, however, and may have exercised some influence on the alignment of churches founded in the

Anglian period, including St Mary Bishophill Junior and the vanished St Gregory's on Barker Lane. After the Anglo-Scandinavian reorganization two short stretches of the Roman road line survived, one inside Micklegate Bar and the other, as excavations have shown, at the north-east end of Tanner Row.

Further examples of Roman street lines which survived into the Anglo-Scandinavian period and beyond may emerge in due course, but it is already clear that the form of the modern city has been substantially determined by decisions about the lines of streets as well as defences taken nearly 2000 years ago and by subsequent adaptations to them. In 71 the foundations were laid for what has since become the great city we know today. There is, however, much still to be learnt about the way that Roman *Eboracum* became modern York, and it is, therefore, in anticipation of many great archaeological discoveries yet to come that I offer this book about its Roman origins to York's citizens and friends.

Sites to visit

York: The Roman fortress

The East Corner. This can be seen, along with interval tower NE6, from the medieval walls. Ascend at Monk Bar in Goodramgate or Layerthorpe Postern on the corner of Jewbury and Peaseholme Green. The precinct in which the remains stand is usually kept locked.

The Multangular Tower and Anglian Tower. They can be seen in the Museum Gardens, along with fine stretches of the fortress wall. Access during daylight hours.

The Principia. Remains of the basilica and finds from the Minster excavations can be seen in the Minster Foundations. Opening hours daily 10.30–16.30.

The Baths Caldarium. Part of the *caldarium* of the baths originally excavated in 1930–1 can be seen in the Roman Bath public house. Access by permission of the landlord.

The Yorkshire Museum. The museum is in Museum Gardens and houses one of the finest collections of Roman antiquities in Britain. There are sculptures, tombstones, inscriptions, mosaics and numerous finds, principally from the cemeteries. Also on display are Roman finds from excavations at Catterick, Stanwick and other sites in Yorkshire. Opening hours daily 10.00–17.30.

Roman Yorkshire

Sites referred to in this book include: *Beadlam Roman Villa*. The remains of one of the excavated buildings can be found in a field *c.* 4 miles from Helmsley on the south side of the A170 Helmsley-Pickering road opposite the turning to Pockley.

Aldborough Roman town. The site is 27 km (17 miles) north-east of York near Boroughbridge. A stretch of defences is visible next to the Museum. Both are in the care of English Heritage. Opening hours as for Scarborough Castle (see below).

Malton Fort and Museum. The fort rampart can be seen in a field on the east side of the road to Pickering *c.* 500 m (550 yds) from the town centre. The museum is in the market place and houses numerous finds from Malton itself and villas in east Yorkshire. Open from Easter to the end of October 10.00–16.00 except Sundays: 12.00–16.00.

Scarborough Signal Station. The remains can be found in the grounds of Scarborough Castle. This site is in the care of English Heritage. Open Good Friday or 1 April (whichever is earlier) to 30 September: daily 10.00–18.00 and 1 October to Maundy Thursday or 31 March (whichever is earlier): Tuesday–Sunday 10.00–16.00 (except 24–26 December and 1 January).

Hull, Transport and Archaeology Museum. The museum is in the High Street and, amongst a large collection of Roman material, there are the mosaics from Rudston villa. Open 10.00–17.00 except Sunday: 13.30–16.30.

Further reading

The starting point for any further reading about Roman York is *Eburacum*, Volume 1 of the inventory of York by the Royal Commission on Historical Monuments (England) published in 1962. The reader may also find some interest and amusement in earlier works including Francis Drake's *Eboracum* (published in 1736), William Hargrove's *History of York* (1818) and Charles Wellbeloved's *Eburacum* (1842). Since 1962 aspects of Roman York have been discussed in *Soldier and Civilian in Roman Yorkshire* edited by R.M. Butler and published in 1971 by Leicester University Press. It includes the following papers which relate specifically to York: Hartley, B., 'Roman York and the northern military command to the 3rd century AD', pp.55–70; Birley, E.B., 'The fate of the ninth legion', pp.71–80; Butler, R.M., 'The defences of the fourth-century fortress at York', pp.97–106; Norman, A.F., 'Religion in Roman York', pp.143–54. In 1984 papers on the archaeology of York appeared in P.V. Addyman and V.E. Black (eds), *Archaeological Papers from York presented to M.W. Barley*, published by York Archaeological Trust. The following are of particular interest for the Roman period: Addyman, P.V., 'York in its archaeological setting', pp.7–21; Brinklow, D.A., 'Roman settlement around the legionary fortress at York', pp.22–7; Ottaway, P.J., '*Colonia Eburacensis*: a review of recent work', pp.28–33; Jones, R.F.J., 'The cemeteries of Roman York', pp.34–42; Sumpter, A.B., 'Interval towers and the spaces between', pp.46–50; Buckland, P.C., 'The "Anglian Tower" and the use of Jurassic limestone in York', pp.51–7.

Detailed publication of recent excavations in York is to be found in the fascicules in the *Archaeology of York* series published for York Archaeological Trust by the Council for British Archaeology. The following concern the Roman period:

Volume 3: *The Fortress*
1. Whitwell, J.B. 1976, 'The Church Street Sewer and an Adjacent Building'.
2. Sumpter, A.B. and Coll, S. 1977, 'Interval Tower SW5 and the South-West Defences: Excavations 1972–75'.
3. Ottaway, P.J., Daniells, M., Hall, R.A., McGregor, H. and Wenham, L.P. (forthcoming), 'Excavations and observations on and adjacent to the defences, 1971–90'.
4. Hall, R.A. (in prep.), 'Excavations at the former City Garage, 9 Blake Street'.

Volume 4: *The* Colonia
1. Carver, M.O.H., Donaghey, S. and Sumpter, A.B. 1978, 'Riverside Structures and a Well in Skeldergate and Buildings in Bishophill'.
2. Ottaway, P.J. and Pearson, N.F. (forthcoming), 'General Accident, Tanner Row and other sites'.

Volume 6: *Roman Extra-Mural Settlement and Roads*
1. Brinklow, D., Hall, R.A., Magilton, J. and Donaghey, S. 1986, 'Coney Street, Aldwark and Clementhorpe, Minor Sites, and Roman Roads'.

Volume 14: *The Past Environment of York*
1. Buckland, P. 1976, 'The Environmental Evidence from the Church Street Roman Sewer System'.
2. Kenward, H. and Williams, D. 1979, 'Biological Evidence from the Roman Warehouses in Coney Street'.

3. Hall, A.R., Kenward, H. and Williams, D. 1980, 'Environmental Evidence from Roman Deposits in Skeldergate'.
5. Kenward, H., Hall, R.A. and Jones, A.K.G. 1986, 'Environmental Evidence from a Roman Well and Anglian Pits in the Legionary Fortress'.
6. Hall, A.R. and Kenward, H. 1990, 'Environmental Evidence from the *Colonia*'.

Volume 15: *The Animal Bones*
3. O'Connor, T.P. 1988, 'Bones from the General Accident Site'.

Volume 16: *The Pottery*
2. Perrin, J.R. 1981, 'Roman pottery from the *Colonia*: Skeldergate and Bishophill'.
4. Perrin, J.R. 1990, 'Roman Pottery from the *Colonia* 2: General Accident and Rougier Street'.

Regular popular accounts of current excavations appear in *Interim*, the quarterly bulletin of the York Archaeological Trust, available for an annual subscription of £4 from 1 Pavement, York, YO1 2NA. Summary annual reports on York excavations also appear in *Britannia*, the journal of the Roman Society.

Local residents and visitors alike will find The Ordnance Survey *Map of Roman and Anglian York*, published in 1988, informative, although in need of some revision as a result of recent work, especially as regards the line of the main road to the south-west and the course of the river Ouse in Roman times.

Other specialist publications on Roman York and related topics are listed under the following thematic headings:

The Fortress and the Roman army in York

Dyer, J. and Wenham, P. 1967, 'Excavations and discoveries in a cellar in Messrs. Chas. Hart's premises, Feasgate, York, 1956', *Yorkshire Archaeological Journal* 39, pp.419–25.
Miller, S. 1925, 'Roman York: Excavations of 1925', *Journal of Roman Studies* 15, pp.176–94.
– 1928, 'Roman York: Excavations of 1926–1927', *Journal of Roman Studies* 18, pp.61–99.
Phillips, D. and Heywood, B. (forthcoming), *Excavations at York Minster* 1 (HMSO).
Radley, J. 1966, 'A section of the Roman fortress wall at Barclay's Bank, St Helen's Square, York', *Yorkshire Archaeological Journal* 41, pp.581–4.
– 1970, 'Two interval towers and new sections of the fortress wall, York', *Yorkshire Archaeological Journal* 42, pp.399–402.
– 1972, 'Excavations on the defences of the city of York in an early medieval stone tower and the successive earth ramparts', *Yorkshire Archaeological Journal* 44, pp.38–64.
Ramm, H.G. 1956, 'Roman York: Excavations of 1955', *Journal of Roman Studies* 46, pp.76–90.
Stead, I.M. 1958, 'Excavations at the south corner tower of the Roman fortress at York, 1956', *Yorkshire Archaeological Journal* 39, pp.515–38.
– 1968, 'An Excavation at King's Square, York, 1957', *Yorkshire Archaeological Journal* 42, pp.151–64.
Wenham, L.P. 1961, 'Excavations and discoveries adjoining the south-west wall of the Roman legionary fortress in Feasgate, York, 1955–57', *Yorkshire Archaeological Journal* 40, pp.329–50.
– 1962, 'Excavations and discoveries within the Legionary Fortress in Davygate, York, 1955–8', *Yorkshire Archaeological Journal* 40, pp.507–87.
– 1968, 'Discoveries in Kings Square, York, 1963', *Yorkshire Archaeological Journal* 42, pp.165–8.
– 1972, 'Excavations in Low Petergate, York, 1957–8', *Yorkshire Archaeological Journal* 44, pp.65–113.
Wright, R.P. 1976, 'Tile stamps of the sixth legion found in Britain', *Britannia* 7, pp.224–35.
– 1978, 'Tile stamps of the ninth legion found in Britain', *Britannia* 9, pp.379–82.

There are also a number of other works which relate to the layout and history of Roman fortresses in Britain. Of particular relevance for the study of York are the following:

Crummy, P. 1984, *Colchester Archaeological Report* 3 (Colchester).
Crummy, P. 1985, 'Colchester: the mechanics of laying out a town', in F. Grew and B. Hobley (eds), *Roman Topography in Britain and the Western Empire*, C.B.A. Research Report 59, pp.78–85.
Henderson, C. 1990, 'Aspects of the planning of the Neronian fortress of *Legio II Augusta* at Exeter', *Exeter Museums Archaeological Field Unit Report* 90.03 (Exeter).
Jones, M.J. 1975, *Roman Fort Defences to AD*

117, British Archaeological Reports, British Series 21 (Oxford).

Pitts, L. and St. Joseph, J.K. 1985, *Inchtuthil*, Britannia Monograph Series 6 (London).

The Colonia

Ottaway, P.J. 1984, 'The *Colonia* at York, past, present and future', in R.F. Jones and P. Wilson (eds), *Settlement and Society in the Roman North* pp.57–64 (Bradford).

Ramm, H.G. 1976, 'The Church of St Mary Bishophill Senior, York: Excavation 1964', *Yorkshire Archaeological Journal* 48, pp.35–68.

Wacher, J. 1975, *The Towns of Roman Britain* (London), especially pages 156–77.

Wenham, L.P. 1965, 'Blossom Street Excavations, York, 1953–5', *Yorkshire Archaeological Jounral* 163, 524–53.

Cemeteries

Wenham, L.P. 1968, 'The Romano-British Cemetery at Trentholme Drive, York', *Ministry of Public Buildings and Works Archaeological Report* 5 (HMSO, London).

Roman Yorkshire

The literature on Roman Yorkshire is extensive, but readers are referred in particular to papers in the British Archaeological Reports, British Series Volume 193 edited by J. Price and P.R. Wilson entitled *Recent Research in Roman Yorkshire*. Papers of particular relevance for York itself include Hartley, B., 'Plus ça change . . . , or reflections on the Roman forts of Yorkshire', pp.153–60; Jones, R.F.J., 'The hinterland of Roman York', pp.161–70; Buckland, P. 'The stones of York: building materials in Roman Yorkshire', pp.237–88.

In addition there are two volumes in the *Peoples of Roman Britain* Series: Hartley, B. and Fitts, L. 1988, *The Brigantes* (published by Alan Sutton) and Ramm, H. 1978, *The Parisi* (published by Duckworth).

The Dalton Parlours villa excavations are published by the West Yorkshire Archaeology Service as S. Wrathmell and A. Nicholson (eds) 1990. 'Dalton Parlours', *Yorkshire Archaeology* Volume 3.

For readers with an interest in the people of Roman York and in Roman inscriptions an excellent introduction is to be found in Birley, A.R. 1979. *The People of Roman Britain*. The same author has written *Septimius Severus: The African Emperor* (1988) which in chapter 16 covers the visit to York.

Glossary

The following Latin terms are used to describe the principal topographical features in the fortress (see also **8**).

intervallum The space between the fortress rampart and the internal buildings.

latera praetorii Literally 'sides of the headquarters' i.e. those parts of the strip of land running across the fortress site which lay on either side of the *principia*.

porta decumana The main gate at the end of the *via decumana*, at York the north-east gate.

porta praetoria The main gate at the end of the *via praetoria*, at York the south-west gate.

porta principalis dextra and *sinistra* The main gates at each end of the *via principalis*, at York the former is the north-west gate and the latter the south-east.

praetentura The area of the fortress in front of the *principia*, at York on its south-west side.

principia The headquarters building.

retentura The area of the fortress behind the *principia*, at York on its north-east side.

via decumana The main street running from the rear of the *principia* to the *porta decumana*.

via praetoria The main street running from the front of the *principia* to the main gate, the *porta praetoria*.

via principalis The main street running across the fortress, at York north-west/south-east, in front of the *principia*.

via quintana The main street running across the fortress, at York north-west/south-east, behind the *principia*.

via sagularis The street running around the fortress defences in the *intervallum* space.

Other Latin terms:

aedes shrine or temple.

Agrimensor (plural *Agrimensores*) Surveyor.

colonia (plural *coloniae*) Literally colony, the term refers to the highest grade of Roman town, populated largely by Roman citizens.

genius Used in the phrase *Genio Loci* meaning to 'the spirit or guardian of the place'.

numen A term used in connection with emperor worship which can be translated as divine power.

opus signinum A form of Roman concrete which includes fragments of tile to improve water-resistant qualities.

pes monetalis (pM) Unit of measurement widely used in York, equivalent to 0.296 m or 0.97 imperial feet. Named after the standard held in the temple of Juno Moneta in Rome.

triclinium (plural *triclinia*) The dining-room in a Roman house.

Index

Page numbers in **bold** refer to illustrations